HE

Für den Bruder
von Be.
R...

22/4/89

ROBERT A. JOHNSON

HE

Understanding Masculine Psychology

*Based on the legend of Parsifal
and his search for the Grail, using
Jungian psychological concepts*

FOREWORD BY RUTH TIFFANY BARNHOUSE

INTRODUCTORY ESSAY BY JOHN A. SANFORD

PERENNIAL LIBRARY

Harper & Row, Publishers
New York, Cambridge, Philadelphia, San Francisco, Washington
London, Mexico City, São Paulo, Singapore, Sydney

HE. Copyright © 1974 by Religious Publishing Co. All rights reserved. Printed in the United States of America. No part of this book may be used or reproduced in any manner whatsoever without written permission except in the case of brief quotations embodied in critical articles and reviews. For information address Religious Publishing Co., 198 Allendale Road, King of Prussia, PA 19406. Published simultaneously in Canada by Fitzhenry & Whiteside Limited, Toronto.

First PERENNIAL LIBRARY edition published 1977. Reissued in 1986.

Library of Congress Cataloging-in-Publication Data

Johnson, Robert A., 1921–
    He : understanding masculine psychology, based on the legend of Parsifal and his search for the Grail, using Jungian psychological concepts.

    "Perennial Library."
    Reprint. Originally published: King of Prussia, Pa.: Religious Pub. Co., 1974. With new introd.
    1. Men—Psychology. 2. Chrétien, de Troyes, 12th cent. Perceval le Gallois. 3. Jung, C. G. (Carl Gustav), 1875–1961. I. Title.
BF692.5.J63 1977   155.3'32   86-45121
ISBN 0-06-097057-X (pbk.)

88 89 90 MPC 10 9 8 7 6 5

Foreword

Women do not really know as much about men as they think they do. They have developed, over the centuries, considerable expertise in the techniques of adapting to men, but that is not the same as truly understanding them. Women often labor under the delusion that life is really pretty easy for men, at least when compared to their own lot, and have no idea what a complicated struggle is really involved in the transition from male childhood to real manhood. They have no idea of the long and arduous road that must be traveled by the male child who *must* separate himself from the original, indispensable, nurturing mother and venture forth into a way of experiencing himself that is not her way and that he cannot learn from her either by example or by instruction. Considered in these terms, it is easy to see that a girl must learn to be like her mother, while a boy must learn to be different from her without this difference deteriorating into either antagonism or fear. Unfortunately, the current conditions of Western culture all too often favor this deplorable outcome, with unfortunate social results.

It is for this reason that the Jungian approach, which tries to look at the enduring core of problems, is so helpful in elucidating the ongoing uproar between men and women. Johnson is particularly successful in explaining very simply, through the creative interpretation of ancient myths (in this case, *Parsifal*), this perennial "war of the sexes."

It might seem to the uninitiated reader that a book which

sets out to elucidate a medieval myth in modern terms would probably be pedantic and dull. Not so! Johnson's style is discursive and friendly, and his very clear expositions of Jungian tenets necessary to explain his approach are slipped painlessly into the body of the text. There is a novelistic sense of suspense, and I am sure that most readers will not be able to put the book down without finishing it. At the same time, once finished, it will be remembered as something well worth going back over, and new insights will surface with each reading.

In short, let me say that I recommend this book highly. It is entertaining, informative, thought-provoking, mysterious, poetic. Men who read it will surely learn much about themselves, and women—particularly those who are unfortunately misled into thinking of men as "the enemy"—will find it a real eye-opener.

RUTH TIFFANY BARNHOUSE, M.D., TH.M.
Assistant in Psychiatry, Harvard University

Mythology and Our Knowledge of God

*An Introduction to the Story
of the Holy Grail*

Mythology was sacred to primitive people; it was as though their myths contained their very souls. Their lives were cradled within their mythology, and the death of their mythology, as happened with the American Indians, meant the destruction of their lives and spirits.

To most modern men, however, the word *myth* is almost synonymous with *falsehood* or *illusion*. This is because of the misguided idea that myths were the childish way ancient man had of explaining natural phenomena that science explains so much better. But certain psychologists and anthropologists are now helping us see myth in another light, to understand that mythology reflects underlying psychological and spiritual processes taking place in the human psyche. C. G. Jung in particular, with his theory of the collective unconscious, has pointed out that myths are spontaneous presenta-

1

tions from the unconscious of psychological and spiritual truths. For Jung, myths have meaning for everyone because they represent in story fashion "archetypes," that is, patterns of life that are universally valid.

A myth stands in relationship to mankind in general as a dream does to the individual. A dream shows the individual an important psychological truth about himself. A myth shows an important psychological truth that applies to mankind as a whole. A person who understands a dream understands himself better; a person who grasps the inner meaning of a myth is in touch with the universal spiritual questions life asks all of us.

Of all the many myths of Western man the story of the Holy Grail is perhaps unique. It is, for one thing, the most recent of all myths. While it draws for its sources upon ancient pagan as well as Christian motifs, the myth of the Holy Grail took shape in the twelfth and thirteenth centuries. Various forms of it appeared almost simultaneously in France, England, Wales, Germany, and other European countries, as though a vast underground life had suddenly broken through into the light. Its Christian content, its recent origin, and its source in the European soil make this legend particularly meaningful to the spiritual situation of modern Western man.

This book had its origin in a series of lectures on the Holy Grail presented at St. Paul's Episcopal Church in San Diego in the spring of 1969 by Robert Johnson. Its treatment of the Grail myth is based on the principles of Jungian psychology. It may be helpful to sketch briefly some of the most important features of that psychology.

A central idea in Jung's psychology is his concept of individuation. Individuation is the lifelong process in which a person increasingly becomes the whole and complete person God intended him to be. It entails the gradual expansion of his or her consciousness and the increasing capacity of the conscious personality to reflect the total self. The ego may be understood as the center of consciousness, the "I" within us, that part of ourselves with which we are consciously identified. The self is the name given to the total personality, the potential person who is within us from the beginning and seeks in our lifetime to be recognized and expressed through the ego.

The individuation process involves the individual in psychological and spiritual problems of great complexity. One difficult problem is always the matter of becoming reconciled with the shadow—the dark, unwanted, dangerous side of ourselves that conflicts with our conscious attitudes and ideals, but with which everyone must somehow come to terms if he or she is to become whole. Rejection of the shadow personality results in a division within the personality and the establishment of a state of hostility between consciousness and the unconscious. Acceptance and integration of the shadow personality are always difficult and painful but result in the establishment of a psychological balance and unity that otherwise would be quite impossible.

Even more difficult is the inclusion by a man of his

unconscious feminine element and by a woman of her unconscious masculine element. One of Jung's great contributions has been his demonstration that each human being is androgynous, that is, combines both masculine and feminine elements. But a man generally identifies with his masculine side and wears his femininity on the inside, so to speak, and a woman conversely. This inner woman in a man Jung calls the anima and the inner man in a woman, the animus.

Inclusion of the feminine element within a man is a matter of great psychological subtlety and difficulty. Yet, unless he accomplishes this, he cannot hope to enter into the full mystery of the self within him. The story of the Holy Grail emerged at a time in history when man's feminine side was beginning to reach consciousness in a new way. The story deals primarily with the difficulty, and importance, of the struggle in a man to make conscious, and relate to, his inner femininity. The Grail legend is for this reason primarily a story of how individuation takes place in a man's psyche. The male reader of this book may find the great landmarks of his psychic life unrolling before him as the story unfolds. Since women have to live with men, however, they too should find the meaning of the Holy Grail legend of great interest, for it will help them understand men at crucial points in their lives.

There is a third problem. The actualization of the self poses a special problem to traditional Christian consciousness. The typical Christian consciousness has been trained for centuries to strive for perfection, the leading of a perfect, blameless life. We are taught, despite the

Gospel, that ultimately God has no patience with our moral or psychological imperfection or darkness. St. Paul is a special offender in this respect. In many places he has made it quite clear that his Christian converts are to be pure, blameless, and holy before God, without anger, rancor, or lust.

The psychology of individuation, however, shows that the goal of this process of becoming whole is not perfection, but completeness. The whole person is never blameless, guiltless, or pure but is one in whom all sides of himself have been combined inexplicably into a total person. This paradoxical unity of the self, which is like a combination of opposites (life is never this *or* that, but both this *and* that), is a secret that cannot be rationally understood or comprehended. Unity is, so to speak, a mystery known only to God. The ego can experience the unity of the self but never logically comprehend it. In Christian language, only by the grace of God can we become whole. Yet, at the same time, a person who would be whole must undergo a great pilgrimage and journey—must search, often painfully, for the ground and fulfillment of his being. It is this mystery of wholeness, which is both the gift of God and the fruit of great effort on the part of man, that is the great theme of the myth of the Holy Grail.

The reader may find his appetite whetted by this book for more reading of this sort. A selected bibliography at the back of the book has suggestions for further reading. For the reader who wants more detailed and scientific knowledge of the psychological background to the legend of the Holy Grail there is Emma Jung's volume *The Grail Legend,* published by G. P. Putnam's Sons for the C. G. Jung Foundation for Analytical Psychology in 1970. The reader will find Mrs. Jung's and Dr. Marie-Louise Von Franz's treatment of the Grail legend complete and rewarding, although no replacement for the shrewd insights into masculine psychology the present book provides.

Thanks are in order to the people of St. Paul's who responded to Mr. Johnson's lectures with such warmth and generosity. Mr. Johnson and I are especially grateful to Glenda Taylor, who transcribed the lectures from tapes into written form; to Margaret Brown, who wrote the synopsis of the story (see the Appendix); and to my secretaries, Gertrude Gridley and Eleanor Garner, who prepared the manuscript for publication. Shall we turn now to the story?

JOHN A. SANFORD
St. Paul's Episcopal Church
San Diego, California

1

Often, when a new era begins in history, a myth for that era springs up at the same time. The myth is a sort of preview of what is to come, and it contains sage advice for coping with the psychological elements of the time.

In the myth of Parsifal's search for the Holy Grail we have such a spiritual prescription for our own time. The Grail myth arose in the twelfth century; many people feel that our modern age began about then, that the ideas, attitudes, and concepts we are living with today had their beginnings in the days when the Grail myth took form.

The theme of the Grail myth was much in evidence in the twelfth, thirteenth, and fourteenth centuries. One hears echoes of it all over Europe. We will be using the French version (see p. 85), which is the earliest written account, taken from a poem by Chrétien de Troyes. There is also a German version by Wolfram von Eschenbach. The English version, *Le Morte D'Arthur*, comes from the fourteenth century; by that time it had been elaborated a great deal. It is enormously complex and has been so editorialized that some of its spontaneous psychological truth has been lost. The French version is simpler, more direct, and nearer to the unconscious; therefore, it is more helpful for our purposes.

It is important to remember that a myth is a living thing and exists within every person. You will get the true, living form of the myth if you can see it as it spins away inside yourself. The most rewarding thing you can do with this or any myth is to see how it is alive in your own psychological structure.

The Grail myth speaks of masculine psychology. We must take everything that goes into the myth as part of man. We will have to cope with a dazzling array of fair damsels, but we must see these too as parts of the masculine psyche. But women also will be interested in the secrets of the Grail myth, for every woman has to cope with one of these exotic creatures, the male of the species, somehow or other—as father, or husband, or son—so I hope it will be helpful for you to observe the incredible carryings-on of the mythological man, Parsifal, and his interior fair maidens.

Our story begins with the Grail castle. The Grail castle is in trouble. The Fisher King, the king of the castle, has been wounded. His wounds are so severe that he cannot live, yet he is incapable of dying. He groans, he cries out, he suffers all of the time. In fact, the whole land is in desolation. The cattle do not reproduce, the crops won't grow, knights are killed, children are orphaned, maidens weep, there is mourning everywhere—all because the Fisher King is wounded.

The notion that the welfare of a kingdom depends upon the virility or power of its ruler has been a common one, especially among primitive people. There are still kingdoms in the primitive parts of the world where the king is killed when he can no longer produce any offspring. He is simply killed, ceremonially, sometimes slowly, sometimes horribly, because it is thought that the kingdom will not prosper under a weak or ailing king.

Now the Grail castle is in serious trouble because the Fisher King is wounded. The myth tells us how this came about. Years before, early in his adolescence, when the Fisher King was wandering around in the woods, he came upon a camp. All the people of the camp were gone, but there on a spit roasting over the fire was a salmon. The boy naively took a bit of the salmon to eat, which is as natural as anything could be. He was hungry, there was the salmon roasting over the fire, and he took a bit of it. Well, he burned his fingers horribly and dropped the salmon. He put his fingers in his mouth to assuage the burn and in so doing got a little bit, a taste, of the salmon in his mouth. But he was badly wounded. He was then named the Fisher King, because he was wounded by a fish.

It is worth looking at the symbolism of this curious set of circumstances, for here we have the first fact of a man's psychology. The salmon is one of the many symbols of Christ. A boy in his early adolescence touches something of the Christ nature within himself, but he touches it too soon, is only wounded by it, and drops it. But notice that he puts his finger in his mouth, gets a little bit of it, and develops a taste that he will never forget. Many psychic wounds in a man come because he touches his Christ nature, that is, his individuation process, prematurely, can't handle it, doesn't see it through, and is wounded by this.

All men are Fisher Kings. Every boy has naively blundered into something that is too big for him, gotten halfway through, realized that he couldn't handle it, and collapsed. Then he is wounded, he is hurt terribly, and he goes off to lick his wounds. A certain bitterness arises in the boy because he tries so hard and actually touches his salmon—his individuation—yet he cannot hold it. It only burns him. If you are to understand any young man past puberty, you must understand this about him. Virtually every boy has to have the Fisher King wound. It is what the church called the *felix culpa*, the happy fault, the happy woundedness.

It is painful to watch a young man become aware that the world is not just joy and happiness, to watch the disintegration of his childlike beauty, faith, and optimism. This is regrettable but necessary. If we are not cast out of the Garden of Eden, there can be no heavenly Jerusalem. In the Catholic liturgy for holy Saturday evening there is a beautiful passage: "Oh, happy fall that was the occasion for so sublime a redemption."

The Fisher King wound may coincide with a specific event, an injustice, e.g., such as when one is accused of something one didn't do. I recall from Jung's autobiography that once his professor read all of Jung's classmates' papers in the order of their merit but didn't read Jung's at all. His professor said, "There's one paper here that is by far the best, but it is obviously a forgery. If I could find the book I would have him expelled." Jung had worked hard on the paper and it was his work. He never trusted that man, or perhaps even the whole schooling process, after that. This was a Fisher King wound for Jung.

According to tradition, there are potentially three stages of psychological development for a man. The archetypal pattern is that one goes from the unconscious perfection of childhood, to the conscious imperfection of middle life, to conscious perfection of old age. One moves from an innocent wholeness, in which the inner world and the outer world are united, to a separation and differentiation between the inner and outer worlds with an accompanying sense of life's duality, and then, hopefully, at last to satori or enlightenment, a conscious reconciliation of the inner and outer once again in harmonious wholeness.

We are now talking about the boy's development from stage one to stage two. One has no right even to talk about the last stage until he has accomplished the second one. It is no good to talk about the oneness of the universe until one is aware of the separateness of the universe. We can do all kinds of mental acrobatics and talk about the unity of all things, which happens to be true, but we haven't a chance of functioning in that manner until we have succeeded in differentiating the inner and the outer worlds. Another way of saying the same thing is that we have to get out of the Garden of Eden before we can even start for the heavenly Jerusalem, even though they are the same place.

The man's first step out of Eden into the pain of duality gives him his Fisher King wound.

The Fisher King wound often disturbs the boy's re-

lationship with other people around him. When a boy
makes the first steps toward individuation, i.e., when
he first touches the salmon, he begins to be somebody
in his own right. But the process is only partly accomplished. That means that he is jarred out of the ordinary
collective; he is no longer a sheep in the herd. His collective relationship with other people and life is de-
stroyed but he hasn't gone far enough, so that he is not
yet an individual who can relate to life in a whole way.
The English expression is that he has fallen between
two stools. He is neither here nor there. So insofar as
one is a Fisher King, one does not relate well. Alienation
is the current term for it. We are an alienated people,
an existentially lonely people; we have the Fisher King
wound.

Read a typical modern novel and you will find that
it revolves around the subject of the lostness and the
loneliness of the alienated man. It is the great subject
now for we are all Fisher Kings. You have only to walk
down the street and look at the faces to see the counte-
nance of the Fisher King. We are all wounded and it
shows.

The myth also tells us that the Fisher King is wounded
in the thigh. You may remember from the Bible that
when Jacob wrestled with the angel he was wounded
in the thigh. The wound in the thigh means that the
man is wounded sexually. One frank version of the Grail
myth has it that the Fisher King was wounded by an
arrow that transfixed both testicles.

But it is not quite adequate simply to say it is a sexual
wound. It is a wound to his maleness, his generative

capacity, his ability to create. That is why the land of the Fisher King is no longer productive, why the cattle won't bear, the crops won't produce. The whole realm is wounded in its generative capacity.

I doubt if there is a woman in the world who has not had to stand by watching her man anguish in his Fisher King aspect. She may be the one who notices, even before the man himself is aware of it, that there is a suffering and a haunting sense of injury and incompleteness in her man. A man suffering in this way is often driven to do idiotic things to cure the wound he carries and ease this desperation that follows him day and night, week in and week out. Usually he seeks an unconscious solution outside of himself, complaining about his work, buying a new car, even getting a new wife, all of which can be his unconscious attempt to heal himself of the Fisher King wound.

So this is the Fisher King wound. The Fisher King lies in a litter and is carried wherever he goes. He groans, he cries, he is in travail. The only time he is happy is when he is fishing. Don't take this too literally; it isn't that the only thing that will cure a man is to go fishing. Rather, fishing is itself a symbol for working with the unconscious, struggling to make conscious that aborted individuation process he stumbled into in his early teens. If a man can relate to the unconscious again it will help him, for his ultimate healing comes only when he completes the process he inadvertently started as a youth.

The Fisher King presides over the Grail castle, where the Holy Grail, the chalice from the Last Supper, is kept. But we are told that the Fisher King cannot touch the

Grail. Because of his wound he cannot be nourished by the Grail, nor be made whole by it, although it is right there in his castle.

How many times have women said to their men, "Look at all the good things you have; you have the best job you have ever had in your life. Our income is better than ever. We have two cars. We have two- and sometimes three-day weekends. Why can't you be happy? The Grail is at hand; why can't you be happy?"

The man is too inarticulate to reply, "Because I am a Fisher King and am wounded and cannot touch any of this happiness."

It is an added hurt that happiness is close at hand but untouchable. The mere fact he has all the things that should make him happy cannot heal the Fisher King's condition, for he suffers from the inability to touch the goodness or happiness already at hand.

Let us continue our story. The court fool (and there is a fool in every good court) had prophesied long before that the Fisher King wound would be healed when a wholly innocent fool arrives in the court. Any good medieval court would understand this. They wouldn't be the least bit disturbed that an innocent fool or youth should be the solution to the problem. So the people of the kingdom wait daily for the innocent fool to arrive and heal their king.

Here the myth is telling us that it is the naive part of a man that will heal him and cure him of his Fisher King wound. It suggests that if a man is to be cured he must find something in himself about the same age and about the same mentality as he was when he was wounded. It also tells us why the Fisher King cannot heal himself and why when he goes fishing it eases his pain but does not cure him. For a man to be truly healed he must allow something entirely different in himself to enter into his consciousness and change him. He cannot be healed if he remains in the old Fisher King consciousness no matter what he does. That is why the young fool part of himself must enter his life if he is to be cured.

In my consulting room a man will sometimes bark at me when I prescribe something strange or difficult for him, "What do you think I am? A fool?" And I say, "Well, it would help."

For it is an innocent and often foolish thing in a man that will begin the cure for him. A man must consent to this. He must be humble enough to look to the young, innocent, adolescent, foolish part of himself to find the beginning of the cure for the Fisher King wound.

2

The myth now turns from the Fisher King and his wound to the story of a boy who doesn't have a name. He was born in Wales. In those days to be born in Wales was to be born in the farthest possible outlands. It is a bit reminiscent of the commentary in the scriptures: "What good could come out of Nazareth?" Apparently Nazareth and Wales were both at the bottom of the list in the collective mind. So, of course, that is where the hero will come from. The hero, the saving quality, comes from the place where you least expect it. We are going to find out later that this boy's name is Parsifal, which means "innocent fool."

It is a humbling thing for a Fisher King to rely on his Parsifal nature for his salvation. It's a bit like the Biblical injunction, "Except ye become as a little child, ye cannot enter the Kingdom of Heaven." Unless you will trust your Parsifal nature for your redemption, there is no hope for you. This comes hard for a man, for his masculine pride bites the dust.

Jung describes an occasion when he was forced to do this. The great falling-out between Jung and Freud occurred over the nature of the unconscious. Freud said that the unconscious is a scrap heap consisting of all the unvalued things in one's life that have been repressed to the unconscious. Jung insisted that the unconscious is also the matrix, the artesian well from which all creativity springs. Freud would have none of this. So the two of them broke. This was a frightening thing for Jung to go through. He was young, untried, with no reputation of his own. It looked as if he were finishing a career almost before it began.

But Jung said he went home and decided that if he really believed that the unconscious was the fountain from which all creativity sprang he would have to trust it. So he locked himself up in his room and waited on the unconscious. It wasn't long before he was down on the floor with his childish games. This led him to recall his childhood fantasies, which he then decided to express in a form of adult play. For months he labored in his backyard, building out of stone the villages and towns and forts he had fantasized as a boy. He trusted his childlike experience, and that was the beginning for him of an outpouring from the collective unconscious, from which we have the legacy of Jungian psychology. That was Parsifal at work.

Parsifal (we will call him that, though he doesn't get a name until much later in the myth) is raised by his mother, whose name is Heart Sorrow. His father is gone, and he knows nothing about him; nor does he have any brothers or sisters. He grows up in primitive circumstances, wears homespun clothes, has no schooling, and is completely untutored. He asks no questions and is just simply a naive youth.

Early in his adolescence he was out playing one day

when five knights came riding by on horseback. Parsifal had never seen a knight before. The scarlet-and-gold trappings, the armor, the shields, the lances, all the accoutrements of the knights dazzle poor Parsifal so completely that he dashes home to tell his mother he has seen five gods. He is on fire from what he has seen and decides to leave immediately to join the five magnificent kings. He hadn't known that such a thing existed.

His mother bursts into tears. She tries to talk him out of it but, wise mother that she is, soon sees that there is no hope, that the boy will go off with the knights. So she tells Parsifal that his father had been a knight and had been killed rescuing a fair maiden. Parsifal's two brothers had also been killed as knights. Parsifal's mother had taken him to a remote place and kept this story from him in hopes that he might not go off to a similar fate. But now it has happened. There is no hope. So she tells him all of this, gives him her blessing, and gives him some instructions. These instructions will reverberate through the whole myth, so it is worth listening to them.

First, she tells him to respect all fair damsels. Second, he is to go to church daily; whenever he needs food he will find it in church. Then she instructs him not to ask any questions, usually pretty good advice to a garrulous boy. But later in the myth we find that this last bit of advice is disastrous.

So Parsifal goes off happily to find his five knights. He never finds these same five knights, but he finds all sorts of other things.

Everyone he meets he asks, ''Where are the five

knights?'' He gets all kinds of answers, all kinds of instructions, all manner of commentaries—all of which are different. And he is bewildered. The five knights are hard to find, for the five knights are everywhere, or maybe the five knights are nowhere. If you look into the eyes of a fourteen- or fifteen-year-old boy who is asking, "Where are the five knights I saw?" and tell him something, you will get that look back. The last person he asked said something different about the location of the five knights. So the five knights are everywhere, but they are also nowhere.

Eventually Parsifal comes to a tent. He had never seen a tent before, for he had grown up in a simple hut, so he presumes that the tent is the cathedral about which his mother had told him. She had said that it would be a magnificent place; well, the tent is the most magnificent place he has ever seen, so he presumes that he has come to God's cathedral. So he bursts into the tent to worship, and he finds a fair damsel. This is the first of a glittering, dazzling, incomprehensible array of fair damsels with which we are going to have to cope.

Parsifal remembers his mother's instructions to treat fairly, to adore, to cherish any fair damsel that he finds. So he proceeds to cherish her by rushing up to her and embracing her. He sees a ring on her hand, takes the ring off, puts it on his own hand, and now has a talisman, a gift from his fair maiden that will be the inspiration for the rest of his life.

Have you ever seen a boy on his first date? This is reminiscent. But of course the fair damsel is insulted.

Parsifal has been told by his mother that he will have

all the nourishment, all the food that he needs for his life, in God's church, and sure enough, there in the tent is a table set for a banquet. The damsel is waiting for her beloved knight who is courting her, and she has spread out the best for him. But to Parsifal, prophecy is working perfectly; here is God's temple, here is the fair damsel, here is everything he could wish to eat. Everything is just as his mother said it would be. Parsifal sits down and eats at the table and decides that life is good.

The damsel by this time is becoming aware that she is in the presence of an extraordinary person. She begins to understand and is not angry, for she realizes that before her is a truly holy, simple, and guileless person. She implores Parsifal to leave immediately, because if her knight comes and finds him in the tent the knight will kill him.

For Parsifal everything is working fine. He has found God's church, he has found a ravishingly beautiful damsel whose ring he now carries. He has been fed; all is well. If you have an adolescent boy, you will recognize all this. It's painful to watch, but beautiful in a way, too.

Parsifal obeys the fair maiden's request to leave and goes on his way. It is not too long before he finds a devastated convent and monastery. The monks and nuns are in travail. The holy Sacrament is on the altar but may not be used; no one can approach it or make use of it. The crops won't grow, the animals won't reproduce, the wells have dried up, the trees bear no fruit, all manner of things have gone wrong. It is a paralyzed land.

Myths often repeat the same theme over and over in different forms, showing a principle at work on many different levels; this is why the situation at the convent and monastery is like that at the Fisher King castle. The devastated land with the Host on the altar that may not be used identifies the situation as a neurotic condition. Though everything one needs is virtually within arm's reach, one can't use it. This is the agonized condition of the neurotic structure of the torn or divided man.

We live in the richest time the world has ever seen. We have more than any people on earth ever had before. Yet sometimes I wonder if we are not also the most unhappy people that were ever on the face of the earth. We are alienated, we are Fisher Kings, we are monasteries over which spells have been cast.

Parsifal sees all this. He doesn't have the strength to cure it on the spot, but he promises to come back when he gets stronger and raise the spell from the monastery. Later on, incidentally, he does return and raise the spell.

3

Now Parsifal continues on his way and is met by a Red Knight who has just come from King Arthur's Court. The Red Knight is so strong that Arthur's court was powerless before him. He simply walked in, took anything he wanted, and did anything he wanted to do. He has in his hands a silver cup, the chalice that he stole from the court.

Parsifal is dazzled by the Red Knight. He has red armor; he has a scarlet tunic; the horse's trappings and saddle and all the knightly equipment are scarlet. He cuts a magnificent figure. Parsifal stops the Red Knight and asks him how he too can get to be a knight. The Red Knight is so perplexed by the naive young fool in front of him that he doesn't harm him but tells Parsifal that if he wants to be a knight, he should go to Arthur's court. Then he laughs and goes on.

So Parsifal finds his way to King Arthur's Court. He tells the first page he meets at the court that he wants to be knighted and asks how this is done.

He is laughed at, of course. The process of becoming a knight is an arduous one. But Parsifal naively asks, and asks, and asks, until finally he is brought to King Arthur himself. Arthur, a kindly man, doesn't scorn

Parsifal, but tells him he must learn a great deal and be versed in all the knightly arts. And Parsifal understands.

Now there is in Arthur's court a damsel who, because of some difficulty that had happened, has not smiled or laughed for six years. The legend in the court is that when the best knight in the world comes along the damsel who has not smiled for six years will burst into smiles and laughter. The instant this damsel sees Parsifal she bursts into laughter. The court is mightily impressed with this. Apparently the best knight in the world has appeared! Here is this naive youth, this boy in homespun garments, completely untutored, and the maiden is laughing. Extraordinary!

We know that until the Parsifal part of a person's nature appears, there is a feminine part of him that has never smiled, that is incapable of being happy, and that she comes to life with a glow when Parsifal appears. If one can wake the Parsifal in a man, another part of him immediately becomes happy.

I had an experience of this recently. A man came to my house and he was crying. Life was just impossible for him. It was not really possible to talk with him. So I told him stories and had him take part in the story. I made him play Parsifal. I made him enter into this childlike journey, and presently he was laughing. The maiden who hadn't laughed for six years burst out in joy in him. Then he had some energy to go on. The awakening of Parsifal in a man sets all manner of living things going in him.

King Arthur takes all this about the maiden laughing very seriously and knights Parsifal on the spot. One of the chamberlains in the court is angry at this and pushes Parsifal into the fireplace, humiliating but not injuring him, and slaps the damsel who had regained her ability to laugh. Parsifal is furious and vows to revenge the insulted maiden.

Then he goes to Arthur and says, "I have a request. I want a horse and I want the armor of the Red Knight." Everyone laughs uproariously, because there had not been a knight in King Arthur's Court who had been strong enough to stand up to the Red Knight. Arthur laughs, too, and says, "You have my permission. You may have the horse and armor of the Red Knight, if you can get it."

Parsifal sets forth. He finds the Red Knight and says that Arthur has given him permission to take his horse and armor. The Red Knight guffaws and says, "Fine, if you can get it."

Parsifal has acquired a page by this time, and the page produces a sword for him. I have never been able to find out where this sword comes from. I am very curious. I would like very much to know where Parsifal's first sword comes from. But I find no reference. He just *has* a sword. Maybe it is a natural sword that a boy has, natively, by inheritance.

So they have a duel, and wonder of wonders, Parsifal kills the Red Knight! He pierces him through the eye.

In the French version, this is the only killing in the myth. Parsifal undoes dozens of knights in the rest of the myth, but he kills only the Red Knight.

The victory over the Red Knight may be accomplished either inwardly, outwardly, or in both dimensions. In any case, the Red Knight represents that strong, virile, masculine stuff a boy needs so desperately.

If the Red Knight is slain outwardly, then the boy gets the masculine virility by overcoming some great obstacle. He defeats or overcomes an adversary in his path in a contest that requires from him courage and risk, and in this way he takes on the power of the Red Knight for himself. Generally such a victory consists in winning something or coming in first in the face of opposition. It may be accomplished by making the football team, or being the best at something, going on an arduous trip such as hiking in the mountains, or defying someone. Unfortunately, a boy generally gets his Red Knight armor by taking it away from someone else. That is the fierce competitiveness of adolescence and masculinity in general. Almost every boy has to win from somebody else. His winning isn't any good unless somebody else loses, which means that he has to lose sometimes, too. But somewhere he's got to get this Red Knight armor. He's got to win, to be top man. Boys will struggle fiercely for this; it is a matter of life and death for them.

Often it takes dozens of Red Knight experiences to get this power. If a man is not careful he will be Red Knighting throughout his life. A man often carries this competitiveness, which has a slightly adolescent tinge to it, into everything. Perhaps some of the lure of battle and war and the glamour of the military life is from the Red Knight structure.

But there is also an inner dimension to the Red Knight struggle. For a boy to become a man he must master

his own aggression. He cannot be a man without knowing how to be aggressive, but it must be controlled
aggression that is at his conscious disposal. If he is just
overcome by his rage and violence, then it is no good;
his masculinity is not yet formed. Psychologically, he
has been defeated inwardly by his Red Knight. His ego
lies prostrate, and the Red Knight in him has won,
emerging as a terrible bully, a violent temper, or even
in vandalism or criminal ways. So every boy on his way
to manhood has to learn how to master this violent side
of himself and integrate that terrible masculine power
for aggression into his conscious personality.

Looked at in this way the Red Knight is the shadow
side of masculinity, the negative, potentially destructive
side. To become truly a man the shadow personality
must be struggled with, but it cannot be repressed. The
boy cannot repress his aggressiveness and win that way,
for he needs exactly that masculine power which is to
be found in his Red Knight shadow. So it is a matter of
his ego becoming strong enough so that he cannot be
overcome by his rage but can use the power in it for
conscious purposes, that is, to overcome obstacles in his
path and achieve his goals.

Obviously the outer battle and the inner battle are
part of the struggle. To win against the outer opponent
and come out top dog a boy must be able to muster and
direct his masculine energies, and also put aside his
cowardice and longing to be protected by mother from
danger. So he cannot win against the Red Knight adversary outside of himself without winning his inner
struggle, too. At the same time, not many boys will win

the struggle just on the inside. That encounter with the outer obstacles which challenges his will and identity is also needed to really firm up his masculinity on the inside.

There is an interesting detail at this moment. When Parsifal is about to put on the Red Knight's armor, his page says, "Take off that awful homespun stuff your mother gave you before you put the armor on." But Parsifal refuses and puts the Red Knight armor over his mother's homespun garment.

In other words, he puts on his new masculinity over his mother complex. Of course, everything goes wrong immediately. This is par for the course for a young man. He takes his newfound strength, his swashbuckling masculinity that he has just discovered at about fifteen or sixteen years of age, and puts it on over his mother complex. That's a laughable combination. Of course, it doesn't work.

So Parsifal gets on the Red Knight's horse and off he goes. There is a wonderful detail in one version of the story that says Parsifal rides all day because he doesn't know how to stop the horse. Somehow by nightfall or from exhaustion, we don't know from what, the horse stops. Parsifal has managed his first day on the horse.

If any man is sufficiently honest with himself, he will remember the first time he got astride the Red Knight's horse and couldn't stop it!

Then Parsifal goes to Gournamond's castle. Gournamond is Parsifal's godfather, so to speak; he trains him, takes some of the rough edges off (among other things Gournamond got his mother's homespun out from underneath the Red Knight's armor), and teaches him the things a boy needs to know for the pursuit of chivalry. He urges Parsifal to stay with him for another year to study, but Parsifal refuses and goes off quite suddenly because he thinks his mother might be in trouble.

Gournamond has taught Parsifal two specific things, and much of the myth revolves around these two instructions. The first is that if Parsifal is to search for the Holy Grail, the only proper pursuit for a knight, one primary requirement lies upon him: He must never seduce or be seduced by a woman. There must be no physical intimacy with a woman, or there is no hope for the Grail.

The second instruction is that when Parsifal gets into the Grail castle he must ask the specific question "Whom does the Grail serve?" This is a curious question, which we do not understand for quite a while, but these two instructions are drummed into Parsifal's head by Gournamond.

So off he goes to hunt for his mother. He finds that soon after he left his mother, she died of a broken heart. You remember that her name was Heart Sorrow. Naturally Parsifal feels dreadfully guilty about this, but this also is part of his masculine development. No son ever develops into manhood without being disloyal to his mother in some way. If he remains with his mother to comfort her and console her then he never gets out of his mother complex. Often a mother will do all she can to keep her son with her. One of the most subtle ways is to encourage in him the idea of being loyal to mother, but if he gives in to her completely on this score then she often winds up with a son who has a severely injured masculinity. The son must ride off and leave his mother, even if it seems to mean disloyalty, and the mother must bear this pain. Later, like Parsifal, the son may then come back to the mother and they may find a new relationship on a new level, but this can only be done after the son has first achieved his independence and transferred his affections to a woman of his own age. In our myth Parsifal's mother had died when he returned. Perhaps she represents the kind of woman who can only exist as mother, who, psychologically, "dies" when this role is taken from her because she does not understand how to be an individual woman, only a mother.

4

So Parsifal never did find his mother again, but it was on this journey that he came upon a fair maiden in distress in the castle of Blanche Fleur. Blanche Fleur is the principal fair maiden of the myth. Everything that Parsifal does after this episode is in the service of Blanche Fleur ("white flower").

Blanche Fleur seems to be the most unsatisfactory female one could imagine, until one remembers that she is not a flesh-and-blood woman. She is part of Parsifal's inner structure, an inner woman. If a flesh-and-blood woman behaved as Blanche Fleur does, one would just write her off immediately.

Blanche Fleur's castle is besieged, so she asks Parsifal to assist her. She promises him the sun, the moon, and the stars if he will help raise the siege of her castle. So Parsifal goes out, finds the second in command of the army besieging the castle, and challenges him to a duel. Parsifal defeats him, gets his pledge of subservience, and sends him off to Arthur's court. Then Parsifal hunts up the first in charge of the besieging army and does exactly the same thing. There will be a whole succession of vanquished knights sent off to Arthur's court before the tale ends.

This battle with the second and first in command may symbolize one of the many battles a boy has to fight to free himself from a father or brother. A boy growing up will go out and fight every member of his family to be free of them, even when he substitutes someone else as a representative of father or brother. Often if there is a sudden flare-up with somebody at work, it is one finishing up some brother things from far back in adolescence.

Having raised the siege, Parsifal goes back to Blanche Fleur's castle and spends the night with her. One receives the most intimate details as to how they spent the night. Summed up briefly, but beautifully, they lay in an embrace, head to head, shoulder to shoulder, hip to hip, knee to knee, toe to toe. But it is a chaste night; they are as brother and sister. This seems hard to believe. But then one realizes that this is an inner meeting, something that goes on inwardly within Parsifal.

For, as we observed, the myth is not talking here about an outer, flesh-and-blood woman when it speaks of Blanche Fleur, but about the man's inner woman, his anima. It is terribly important to make this distinction between the outer, flesh-and-blood woman and a man's inner feminine quality, and to keep inner laws differentiated from outer laws. The laws of the psyche, the laws that pertain inwardly, are unique and often different from the outer laws. The matter of what to do with the inner woman, and especially how to differentiate her from the outer woman, is the most important part of the myth.

So it is very important to understand this strange injunction that a man is not to have a carnal relationship with any woman if he is to find the Grail. This is the most important thing in the whole Grail myth. If we can understand it, we will have a jewel in our hands.

Again, please remember that this is a set of instructions on how a man shall manage or relate to his interior feminine woman, his anima; it has nothing to do with how a man relates to a flesh-and-blood woman. People don't usually know this. They don't have this dimension available for thinking. Therefore, they apply the injunction outwardly, and the myth, the medieval ages, and the whole movement of chivalry are largely misunderstood.

One is no closer to happiness or the Grail by leaving flesh-and-blood woman alone. When we take this inner law and try to apply it outwardly, we end up being puritanical and guilt-ridden, which practically all of us are, and we still have no laws for our inner conduct. There is little information in the Grail myth about what to do with flesh-and-blood women, but there is a great deal about what to do with that inner woman. That is the information we need so badly.

One can think of many spiritual things that are negated by taking them outwardly instead of inwardly. The virgin birth is one. This has a powerful meaning for anyone who is going through the individuation process, for it tells us that the miraculous event, the birth of Christ within us, comes about through the intercourse of divine powers with the eternal human soul. That Christ birth can come in us, too, if our soul interacts with God, and when it does it is just as miraculous and unbelievable as a virgin birth. But if we get stuck in the literal, historical question—did it happen literally that way with Jesus' human birth—then we never get to this inner meaning and its profound truth.

Much of Christianity is a set of laws for relating to, coping with, or making meaningful the inner parts of one's being, not a set of laws for outer conduct. Few people are aware of this differentiation.

If we confuse these laws—inner and outer—we really have a difficult thing going. If a man treats a flesh-and-blood woman according to the laws that would be appropriate for his own interior femininity, his anima, there is just chaos.

Look at what happened in the Middle Ages, when men first really began to cope with the anima. The anima has always been there, but it is only recently that man has had the capacity to come to any kind of conscious relationship to his own femininity. Before that, everything was lived out instinctively with the flesh-and-blood women around him. It was when man began to come to sense the difficulty of the anima and her danger to him that all the witch hunts started. Instead of quelling the interior feminine, which was the dangerous one, he had to go out and burn some poor creature who was behaving a little strangely. We are just getting to the point now where we can burn the right woman, namely, the interior one (although burning her is not too good a practice in any case; she will turn around and burn you if you do). We haven't really gone very far past the witch hunts yet. We are still projecting onto outer, flesh-and-blood women our relationship, or lack of it, to our inner femininity.

The laws of chivalry say that one should be chivalrous to a woman, not touch her, but treat her as if she were the queen of heaven. But chivalry doesn't make much sense in dealing with actual, flesh-and-blood women. There are, of course, outer laws, too. The outer woman merits the greatest respect and tenderness, but she will be most unhappy and things will not go well if a man confuses her with his inner woman.

To learn more about how the inner woman affects a man, we must make some important distinctions between emotion, feeling, and mood. Most people lump these experiences together indiscriminately. For them, a mood is an emotion and a feeling. We must not do this, for the distinctions to be made between these experiences enable a man to distinguish his inner woman and help him see clearly the way she operates in his psychology. So we will spend some time on this.

Emotion is a sum of energy that occurs, or is set off, in a person by a meaningful experience. Its chief characteristic is its energy. Emotion itself is morally neutral; it may be good or it may be destructive, depending on where and how it is invested. To be really excited about something can bring much emotion, and it can sustain some beautiful things in one's life. There is also much emotion involved in depression: One is wringing one's hands or walking circles on the rug, hunting for something to be miserable about. Emotion defined as energy is relatively easy to understand.

It is more difficult to describe feeling. This is a word that is used far too generally and imprecisely, and therefore it almost loses its usefulness. I am going to use the word *feeling* in a precise way to describe a specific experience. Feeling is the act of valuing. It is not necessarily hot and volatile like emotion, but it is that rational faculty which assigns value to an experience. This is the sense in which Jung uses the term in his definition of thinking, feeling, sensation, and intuition.

One thinks about something, makes an intellectual appraisal of it, understands it, but by so doing there is not yet feeling about it. There is no sense of judgment nor any valuation, so one has not related to it yet. The act of thinking is quite different from the act of feeling. To feel is to assign value to an experience. If asked, then, how one feels about something, the proper answer would be that it feels good or bad, terrible or beautiful. Thus we place a value on something by feeling.

Then there is mood. This is a thorny one, for mood is a strange thing. It is like a small psychosis, or possession. A man's mood comes from being overpowered by the feminine part of his nature. Mood is beautifully described in Hindu mythology as Maya, goddess of illusion. Mood is being overwhelmed or possessed by some interior feminine content in one's unconscious. When seized by a mood, it is as though a man has become an inferior woman. Modern slang puts it aptly: He just becomes bitchy, that's all.

It is a rare man who knows very much about his inner feminine component, his anima, or who has much relationship with it. It is fair to say that if a man undertakes any inner development, it is essential that he discover his anima, put her in a bottle, so to speak, and put the cork in. He will need to take her out again, but first he has to learn not to be controlled by her moods and affects or led by her seductions. Of course, putting the cork in the bottle is only the first step in dealing with the anima. The later and far more important step is to learn to relate to her, to have her as an inner feminine companion who will walk with the man and warm his life for him. Ultimately the man has only two alternatives: Either he rejects this feminine side and it turns against him in the form of bad moods and undermining seductions, or he accepts it and relates to the feminine side of himself and of life and it gives him warmth and strength.

Some men seem to have an enormous anima potential; that is, they just have more of the feminine within themselves. This is neither good nor bad in its own right. If they can bring this feminine side to good development, then they can be highly creative men and no less masculine just because of their powerful inner feminine component. These are the artists, the seers, the intuitive, sensitive men who are so culturally valuable in any society. But if they cannot come to terms with that interior woman, she will run them and probably destroy them before she is done with it. Any woman who is rejected turns negative, and the inner woman of a man is no exception.

A man's relationship to his anima shows on his face. You need only walk down the street and look at the men you pass to get an immediate sense of their relationship to the anima. A man with no relationship to his feminine side either looks hard and inflexible and bitter, or eaten away on the inside. There is a story about Lincoln, who, after an interview with somebody, said to his secretary, "I don't like that man's face." The secretary said, "But he can't help what his face is; he is not responsible for his face." Lincoln replied, "After forty every man is responsible for his face."

5

Let's return now to the difference between *feeling* (one's ability to value) and *mood* (one's being overtaken or possessed by an inner feminine content). If a man has a good relationship to his anima, his inner femininity, he is able to feel, to value, and thus to find meaning in his life. If a man is not related to his anima, then he can find no meaning and has no capacity for valuation. So here is a sharp collision between the two kinds of interior experience a man goes through.

What the Grail myth is telling us is that in his relationship to the interior feminine a man should relate to her, that interior woman, on a feeling level and not on a mood level. Parsifal is instructed to relate to Blanche Fleur, i.e., to his anima, in the feeling sense, which is a noble and useful and creative sense, not in a seductive sense, which is destructive. Not to seduce or be seduced, which are forbidden if one is to find the Grail, means not to fall prey to a mood. As soon as a man gets into a mood, he has no capacity for relationship, no power to feel, and therefore no capacity for valuation.

Any woman knows this. When her man gets into a mood, she might just as well give up for the day, or at least the hour, because he is just not available. He is not available for relationship when he is in a mood, even a good mood. Good moods are fun, but they are still a form of possession. The goddess Maya, the goddess of illusion, does nothing but evil. Any time that wooing goddess Maya appears, all reality, all objectivity, all creativity is put to an end. Or, in terms of our myth, if you seduce or are seduced by a fair damsel, i.e., the anima, your chances at the Grail are finished. Myths and dreams overstate their case. So I don't think one's chance at the Grail is gone forever, but it's gone for the time being. If a man is seduced by his anima, if the goddess Maya gets hold of him and weaves her spell, he is done. He cannot think, he cannot function, he cannot relate. He thinks he is doing a great deal and much churning is going on inside him, but he is virtually out of commission until the mood is over or until he sheds it.

You know what happens when a man gets in a mood: Everything is colored by the mood he is in. If he wakes up in the morning "on the wrong side of the bed," i.e., if the mood has got him, then everything looks bad. He knows before he gets to the morning paper that the stock market is down. He doesn't have to look out the window to tell it is raining. He is sure that all manner of things are wrong, and if they are not wrong, he will make them wrong. He imprints on outer reality the character of this mood in which he is caught. His mood tends to be infectious, too, and pretty soon he has his wife and children upset if they are not wise to what is going on.

This is particularly true of his wife, for she feels

somehow that she is responsible for her husband's bad mood. *What have I done?* she thinks to herself. The fact that her husband may think she is responsible also does not help her any. In her anguish she may do all the wrong things—like assaulting her man with her animus, her masculine side. She feels compelled to break through that mood somehow and find her man and find out what is going on. But, of course, it all turns out badly and usually results in a battle royal between the man's moody woman and the woman's angry man. That is the worst kind of fight, between the feminine side of a man and the masculine side of a woman, because the two are totally possessed. That is when the really dark things happen. But it need not be that way if the woman can remember that it isn't her fault that her man is in such a bad way. His mood is his problem, and if she just retires to the sidelines for a while and stops feeling so guilty, he may come out of it.

One of the first characteristics of a mood is that it robs us of all sense of meaning. Relatedness is necessary if we are to have a sense of meaning or fulfillment. If something is wrong with one's ability to relate, the meaning in life is gone. So *depression* is another term for mood. One finds that most of the content of a psychosis is the anima for a man. It is a flooding, a possession. So a mood is a little madness, a slight psychosis that overtakes one.

Have you ever bought something, then looked at it next day and said, "What in the world?" This is what a mood can do. For a man will get wildly enthusiastic about that new piece of fishing equipment or a new gadget for the boat. The anima seizes upon highly impractical things: fishing gear, the latest nylon leaders, luxurious cars, or something like that. This is anima territory. If you watch, a man simply whips up a storm over this thing, although you know that next week it will be as dead as a mackerel. So much money gets spent, so much energy is lost by moods. I doubt if there is a household around that hasn't shelves piled high with the results of anima attacks, of good moods that carry us away.

Now you can't say a man should do this or shouldn't do that. A man can get out his fishing gear on a Saturday afternoon and have a perfectly fine time and be refreshed by it. Then the next Saturday afternoon he can take out all of his gear and have a perfect anima attack over it. It is not the gear; it is whether or not something has hold of him. It is the anima contamination that makes the difficulty.

A man is not master in his own house when he is in a mood. He is being run and is impossible to live with. He is also terribly critical of the nearest woman he can lay hands on. Something in him knows that the woman in him, the interior woman, is dangerous. So he criticizes his wife, of course, since he knows nothing of the inner woman.

Gournamond told Parsifal he should neither seduce nor be seduced. Not only is one seduced by the anima, he may also try to seduce the anima. When it is said that one is not to seduce his interior fair maiden, I think it means that one must not ask for the good moods. He must not rape his feminine side. He may ask for fulfillment, but he may not ask for the good moods.

Here is a differentiation that most people are incapable of until they achieve some psychological understanding. That exuberant, top-of-the-world, bubbling, half-out-of-control mood which is often so highly prized among men is a dangerous thing: It too is a seduction. The man has seduced the anima. He has it by the throat and has said, "You are going to make me happy or else." This is plain seduction. And he pays a big price for it later, for the law of compensation says a depression must come later to reestablish the balance.

I learned a long time ago not to mortgage experience ahead of time. If I am going to try to get away from it all on Monday, I have to keep my hands off it or I will wreck it before I get there. That would be a seduction of the anima. If I start wringing some pleasure out of it, especially in advance, I will ruin it.

This is an American sport. We think it is our God-given right to be happy, in the sense of mood happiness, and it just doesn't work. I know two boys who planned a camping trip. Gloriously, for days ahead, they planned how great this was going to be. All the mood characteristics arose. Bits of equipment suddenly became Holy Grails. They marveled at the sharpness of this knife or the efficiency of that bit of rope. These fellows milked all the happiness out of that experience ahead of time. I found out that they went to Lake Tahoe, fooled around for half a day, couldn't think of a thing to do, got into the car, and came home. There was nothing there. They had seduced the whole life out of it in advance.

We Americans demand good moods. We think it is

our God-given right to reach out and get something out of that wench inside us. And this is where we so often get into trouble, for when our expectations are disappointed we fall into a foul mood instead.

Some men try to live in an almost perpetual mood. That is very exhausting. I will never forget the day when it first dawned on me that I didn't have to give way to a mood. This was a revelation. I thought one came down with a mood as one came down with a cold. He just bore it and saved other people as well as he could. But we can do better than that.

It is highly advantageous for a man to know enough and to be wise enough so that he can refuse a mood, or at least postpone it. One simply does not have to fall prey to one of these vaporous, Maya-like emanations from the unconscious. A mood creeps up sometimes, and one doesn't know what in the world it is. Things just begin to turn gray. Well, don't accept it. Don't be seduced by it. Don't go down into that quicksand. It is very beguiling and it is so easy just to fall into, but we don't have to if we know what is happening to us.

If a person is ill, he is more subject to moods. His physical strength is not so great, so he is more vulnerable. But still it is not necessary to fall into a mood. One may not feel well and not be happy; there is no dishonor in this. But we don't have to get into a blue funk and get moody over it, although admittedly it is more difficult when we are ill.

Sometimes outer circumstances, especially a woman who is out to get a man's goat, make it very hard for a man to stay out of a mood. But it is still the man's re-

sponsibility to know what is going on within him so he
does not become possessed. A man who has this kind
of self-knowledge begins to develop ego strength. A
man is virtually helpless in his moods because he is a
child in the face of his inner woman. He doesn't want
psychological knowledge because he wants to be taken
care of. It takes a strong man to stand firm against a
mood, and this means a man who is freeing himself of
his childishness, i.e., his mother complex.

Now we should mention another term: *enthusiasm.*
There is a fine but important difference between mood
and enthusiasm. The word *enthusiasm* is a beautiful
word. In Greek it means "to be filled with God." It is
one of the most sublime words in the whole English
language. If one is filled with God, a great creativity
will flow, and there will be a stability about it. If one is
filled with the anima, one may also feel creativity, but
it will probably be gone before nightfall. One must be
wise enough to know the difference between God and
the anima; most men aren't. You can't even tell by looking at another person whether he is swept off his feet
illegitimately and destructively, or whether this is some
of God's laughter welling up through him and is a
beautiful thing. We say a person is in a good mood. If
we mean he is genuinely happy, this is a noble thing.
Laughter is positive and creative, unless it comes from
a mood. It is the level within the man from which
laughter, and what seems to be happiness, springs that
puts its stamp on it. If he is anima-possessed at that
moment, if he has been seduced by a fair damsel, then
there is trouble.

One can sense this in a person. If it is a nervous, tense, taut kind of thing, then there is probably a seduction going on, and he will pay for it and very likely make everyone within earshot pay for it too before he is finished. If it has a beautiful quality to it, if he is at ease with it, it is probably a legitimate happiness that is rushing through him; don't begrudge it to him then.

Generally a mood will run its course in an intelligent man; if a woman doesn't puncture it prematurely, the man will puncture it himself. He will regain his senses somewhere along the way; he will say, "Now, wait, maybe we had better think about this." That is, if his wife hasn't said five minutes before, "Now, dear, don't you think we had better think about this?" Because then he won't, of course.

If a woman is needling, it is doubly hard for a man to come out of a mood. That intensifies it. A man is really in a kind of travail when he is in a mood. He needs help, not needling, but feminine help. He probably won't thank you for it, but inside he will be awfully grateful.

When a woman has to deal with a man in a mood, she generally does the wrong thing. She generally gets her animus out, that critical thing, and says, "Now, look, this is utter nonsense, stop it. We don't need any more fishline leader."

That is just throwing gasoline on the fire. There will be an anima-animus exchange and all will be lost. The two are in the right hand and in the left hand of the goddess Maya and you might as well give up for the afternoon.

There is, however, a point of genius that a woman can bring forth if she is capable of it and willing to do it. If she will become more feminine than the mood attacking the man, she can dispel it for him. But this is a very, very difficult thing for a woman to do. Her automatic response is to let out the sword of the animus and start hacking away. But if a woman can be patient with a man and not be critical, but represent for him a truly feminine quality, then, as soon as his sanity is back sufficiently for him to comprehend such subtleties, he will likely come out of his mood.

A wife can help a great deal if she will function from her feminine side in this way. She has to have a mature femininity to do this, a femininity that is strong enough to stand in the face of this spurious femininity the man is producing. For one thing, the man very likely will project everything onto her and be absolutely sure he is married to a witch and that his bad mood is all her fault. Maybe she is nagging, but he must reckon with his inner woman instead of with her.

It is in the nature of the anima and animus in their primitive form (and that's where most of us are) to live in projection. So when a man's in a mood, he usually says it is his wife bedeviling him. If a man's inner woman is on a rampage, he will likely have the outer woman in a rampage whether she agrees to it or not. On the other hand, if a man is in good relation to the inner woman, then he gets on well with the outer woman, too.

A woman is much more in control of her moods. She can use them. She tries them on and sees which one she is going to wear. She will even change in midstream if necessary. A man doesn't have as much control over his moods; in fact, he has almost no control. Many women are masters of the whole feeling department as few men ever are. Much difficulty arises because a woman presumes that a man has the same kind of control over his mood that she does over hers, but he doesn't. She must understand this and give him time, or help him a little bit.

Women who have to deal with the exotic creature called the male of the species should be easy on him when he is in a mood, because he is nearly helpless in the face of it. He needs help. If there is one rule that should be understood in marriage, it would be that when a man is falling into a mood the woman should withhold all judgment and criticism for the moment if she possibly can. Then, later, when the man is himself again, they may be able to discuss together what was bothering him so much. Waiting like this is hard for a woman to do, of course, but if she remembers that the mood is basically his problem, and not her fault, then she can usually find the wisdom to wait for the right moment to see what the problem is.

As for the man, he cannot realistically expect never to succumb to a mood, but he can remember, even when he is possessed by it, that he is being taken over by something. A man is in partial control if he can just say to himself, "I'm having an anima attack." If he can also say to his wife, "I'm in a bad mood. It's not your fault. Just leave me alone for a while," then he will do her a big favor, and that very act will begin to free him. For

the battle is half won as soon as the man recognizes
that it is a mood which is possessing him.

Parsifal and Blanche Fleur are examples of the whole
matter going rightly. Blanche Fleur is the ultimate of
beauty and inspiration for Parsifal. Nothing goes wrong
for these two. This is the ideal anima relationship. So
if you want to learn how to get on with that curious
inner feminine quality, study the relationship of Parsifal
and Blanche Fleur. She is his lady. He does everything
from here on in the myth for her.

Goethe came to the astounding observation late in
his life that the province of man is to serve woman;
then she will serve him. He was talking about the inner
woman, the muse. She is the carrier of the beauty, the
inspiration, the delicacy of the whole feminine side
of life. It is beautiful, each serving the other back
and forth.

I've been reading a rash of articles lately on the new
feminism that disturbs me because so much of it is
woman demanding to come out of her traditional feminine role of serving man. She is coming out of her slav-
ery. In some respects this is necessary, but in some other
respects it could be nearly fatal. Each should serve the
other. This is the ideal. We can't do without it. One
cannot live without the service, without the love, without the nurturing and the strength of the other.

Parsifal understands this, and he makes a correct relationship with Blanche Fleur. He is devoted to her; he
lies with her, head to head, toe to toe, but he does not
seduce her nor is he seduced by her. He is strengthened
by her. He is devoted to her. He serves her. He is close

to her. There is no prohibition against a closeness to one's interior feminine—the closer, the better. But there must be this fine differentiation: no seduction or the Grail is lost. Parsifal succeeds in this.

6

Our story continues. We left Parsifal at Blanche Fleur's castle after he had freed her. He is still guilt-stricken over what he has done to his mother. Remember, he left quite suddenly and she died of a broken heart.

It is interesting that almost every time Parsifal makes a bit of an advance or when something important has happened, he is suddenly concerned with his mother. A boy must become strong before he can look at his mother, his parents, or his family situation with any kind of objectivity, even to write postcards home and be civil. If a boy divests himself a little of his mother complex, there is the beginning of a chance he might relate with his mother. But he must get a little strength first and become an independent man.

As soon as Parsifal has gotten a little strength from Gournamond and Blanche Fleur, he thinks again of his mother. But as we will see, it is basically his mother involvement that makes all the trouble. This is the greatest stumbling block that exists in a man's psychology. Almost no man will admit it, which means that he is probably totally eaten up by it. But as a man grows, he has a chance to make a better relationship with his mother complex. At every point of growth in the Grail myth, Parsifal turns around to redo his mother relationship.

Parsifal has traveled all day after leaving Blanche Fleur. At nightfall he has no place to stay. He is far out in the woods. He passes by somebody who says there is no habitation within thirty miles. But just at dusk he comes across two men in a boat. One is fishing, the other rowing. The fisherman invites him to come and stay with him for the night. He gives Parsifal directions to his house and goes on.

Parsifal follows the instructions and finds himself at a moat with a drawbridge over it. He scarcely has ridden over the drawbridge when it is pulled up, actually striking the back feet of his horse as it snaps closed.

Parsifal finds himself in a great castle. As he goes into the courtyard, four youths come out, take his horse, take off his clothes, bathe him, and dress him in beautiful scarlet clothing. Then two youths lead him to the fisherman he has seen, who is, of course, the Fisher King. The Fisher King apologizes because he is wounded and therefore unable to rise and greet Parsifal properly. But the whole court is there—400 knights and their ladies. There is a fireplace in the center of the great hall that faces in each of the four cardinal directions.

One learns that in symbolism when the number four appears, it signifies the presence of completeness or totality. This is the Grail castle. If we hadn't known it any other way, we could tell by the many symbols of totality that turn up—the four youths, the 400 knights and ladies, the four faces of the fire.

So the Fisher King, groaning in agony, welcomes

Parsifal. There is some ceremony, and then a procession comes in. A youth carries a sword that drips blood constantly. Then a maiden comes bearing the chalice, the Holy Grail itself. Another maiden comes bearing the paten that was used at the Last Supper. There are many more things in the procession, but these are the ones with which we are mainly concerned.

A great banquet is held. The Fisher King presides from his couch. He can't even sit up. As the Grail is passed about without a word, it gives each guest whatever food he silently wishes for. He has only to wish, and the Grail produces the food or drink. A silver tray does likewise.

As the evening goes on, Parsifal is dazzled by what is happening. The Fisher King's niece brings a sword and gives it to the Fisher King, who straps it onto Parsifal's waist. It becomes Parsifal's sword. Parsifal is speechless at this gift.

You can imagine this country boy in a castle with all this ceremony going on, especially the magic of the Grail. Parsifal says not a word.

Remember Gournamond told him that when the true knight comes to the Grail castle, if he is lucky enough to find it, he must ask the great question, "Whom does the Grail serve?" But Parsifal is remembering the advice of his mother, "Don't ask questions," so he keeps absolutely still. He is just amazed at everything that is going on. He relapses into complete naiveté and simply observes.

The evening wears on. The Fisher King is carried in his litter to his own room, and all the guests and knights depart. Two youths take Parsifal to his quarters, undress him, and put him to bed.

In the morning when Parsifal wakes there is not a soul to be seen. He knocks on several doors, but there is no response. He goes down into the courtyard. His horse is saddled and ready. He calls. Empty echoes. No one is about. He gets on his horse and goes over the drawbridge. Again the drawbridge snaps closed, striking the back feet of the horse. Then the Grail castle disappears. There is nothing but forest.

Now let's pause and see where we are. The Grail castle is the place of the most precious feminine quality, and the Grail is the epitome of all that is feminine. It is the highest feminine symbol, the holy of holies in its feminine expression. It is that for which the knight searches all his life. It gives a man everything that he asks even before he asks it. It is perfect happiness, the ecstatic experience.

The thing that is most touching about this part of the myth is that it is telling us that a youth can blunder into the Grail castle sometime in his midadolescence without earning it or even asking for it. Perhaps every boy in his adolescence spends at least one day in the Grail castle and experiences this perfection.

The first two sentences in a book I received today read: "All of us at some moment have had a vision of our existence as unique, untransferable, and very precious. This transformation almost always takes place during adolescence." There it is.

Usually a man has repressed this, but if he will remember back, somewhere there was a moment when he stumbled into the Grail castle. This usually happens around fifteen or sixteen years of age. There is that morning or that perfect day. One wakes up in the middle of the night and goes out and walks in the moonlight. It is not a love affair at this time, but is often closely associated with the first falling in love.

It is a solitary experience. It may happen among others, but basically it is a solitary experience. I remember a boy who told me that he woke up one summer morning when he was fifteen, climbed out the window, and went out to watch the sunrise. Then he climbed in the window again, woke up, and came down to breakfast as though nothing had happened. But he had been in the Grail castle for that couple of hours in the early dawn.

Some people are wise enough, courageous enough, or honest enough to record these events. Poets speak of such mornings early in life when they discover beauty, ecstasy, the golden world.

The Grail castle doesn't exist physically. It is an inner reality, an experience of the soul. I think it is probably best described as a level of consciousness; a boy wakes up with something new in him—a power, a perception, a strength, a vision. This is his Grail castle. He can't describe it or hang onto it, but he will never be the same again.

People often tease an adolescent out of his Grail castle experience, but one should never do this. It is a holy thing for him. Nothing will ever happen to him that is more beautiful, or more important, or more formative for him.

For when he is out of the Grail castle he is miserable. He can think of nothing else. Nothing else will do once he has seen the Grail castle. Even if he represses the memory of the Grail castle from his consciousness, his longing for it will eat away at him from the unconscious.

There is an old proverb from the Middle Ages that a person has a chance at the splendor of God, at the golden world, twice in his life—once early in adolescence and again when he is forty-five or fifty. Parsifal will come back to the Grail castle years later and ask the right question. This time he only blundered into it and he can't cope with it. No boy can cope with the Grail experience when it first comes to him. He can't stand it. But he does see it. He is touched, almost fatally, by it. It sometimes destroys him. More often than not it fires him up to a wild, compulsive kind of search. It is the motivation, conscious or unconscious, for a great deal of the rest of his life, for in the Grail castle he has known perfect happiness. He has known that utter, absolute contentment, and beauty, and joy that the Grail castle can give him. Then when he loses it all, he becomes a Grail searcher, an urgent, questing beast, fairly pawing the earth to find again the beauty he viewed so briefly. His spiritual hunger forces him to climb everything that is climbable, to try this, to try that, in a restless search for the lost Grail castle. The Grail gives complete satisfaction and wholeness. If you have ever had that, how can you live an ordinary life?

Parsifal could not stay in the Grail castle because he failed to ask the question Gournamond had told him to ask. He remained silent because he followed his mother's advice and not Gournamond's. His mother complex cost him the ability to stay in the Grail castle.

A man's mother complex does not allow him to stay in the Grail castle the first time around. After a man is out of his mother's grip, as soon as he will ask the question in the Grail castle, then he can live in it.

If the Grail castle experience is very strong for a boy, it nearly incapacitates him. The youths who wander around seemingly without any motive or idea where they are going are sometimes young men who have been half-blinded by their Grail castle experience.

Most men find it all so difficult, so painful, so incomprehensible that they immediately repress it, and say, "I don't remember it." But like all repressed things in the unconscious, far from having gotten rid of it, we find it is everywhere, behind every tree and every door, looking over the shoulder of every person we see.

So much of the boy's bantam rooster behavior is a turning off of the Grail castle experience. It hurts so much he can't stand it, and he tries to persuade himself he is very tough to get away from the pain.

Grail hunger accounts for all kinds of things. It's terrifying to approach this hunger in ourselves. If a man is courageous enough, he will understand the hunger I am talking about. It is a hunger that has to be filled. He's got to have something, he's not sure what. It is the Saturday-evening restlessness of a youth. He has to have something or he will explode.

Much advertising plays upon this hunger in a man. I am not sure how conscious advertising people are about it, but they know how to play on this. You can sell a man almost anything if you indirectly call it the Grail.

This is also part of the reason at least for the incredible hunger of people today for drugs. That is a magical way of getting back to the Grail ecstasy. Drugs will take you to an ecstatic experience, but I think it is the wrong way. The right way doesn't necessarily take a long time, but it is a long way. There are no shortcuts. The Grail experience is dangerous. As we said, too much of it or the experience of it at the wrong time is an invitation to a psychotic experience. The drawbridge can click shut too soon, and one is trapped and cannot get out.

It is terrible to observe, but it is true of almost any man that if he thinks something will fill that Grail quest in him, no cost is too high. If he were to die the next morning, he still would do it if it promised to fill that Grail hunger. It is an irrational thing that knows almost no bounds. Much of the motivation of late adolescence—the derring-do, the ninety-miles-an-hour down the highway, or drugs even if it wrecks him—is the unconscious hungering for the Grail.

A boy almost always misconstrues this eruption of his feeling life. He translates it into a mood, which is partly a protective device, but it only makes trouble. He has to solve the mood problem before he can get on with the quest. Many boys are immobilized by the mood life and never change. The whole Grail quest gets sidetracked into a mood experience. The boy eventually becomes only a crotchety old man.

It is almost a universal consensus among philosophers and poets in the Western world that life is tragic. *Tragedy* is a good term for what we are observing. Man in his Grail quest is the tragic man. The word *tragedy* has come to mean the quest for what one cannot attain or have. That is Western man, and that applies to the Grail castle. In the middle part of life, we are hungry for something that we cannot have. This is the tragic dimension of life.

If a man is really honest and you come up to him and ask him how he is, he may say, as one man very honestly said to me once, "Well, Robert, I am turning the crank."

Middle age is the time in between the two Grail castle visits. He is proceeding, he is doing his duty; he is getting the mortgage paid off, getting the kids through school, and keeping his job going. But he is not satisfied, for deep within himself is the hunger for the Grail castle.

One looks to see the parallel in a girl's life. She never leaves the Grail castle. This is another thing one must understand about men. Women keep a sense of beauty, a sense of connectedness, a sense of at-homeness in the universe that a man doesn't have. I don't think a man is more creative than a woman. But his creativity comes in a different form. The pressure, the emergency quality of a man's creativeness comes because a man leaves the Grail castle. A woman discovers what always is, and a man goes out and makes or creates afresh—or thinks he does.

Einstein was quoted as saying, "I now bask in that solitude which was so painful to me in my youth." The loneliness, the feeling of pressure in a man is the hurt of his Grail experience. To have seen something so beautiful and then to be without it is nearly unendurable.

Many men try to make a flesh-and-blood woman fill this loneliness. They try to make an outer woman into the Grail for them. This doesn't work because they are trying to make her into something that she cannot possibly be. This is asking something outer to fill an inner need.

The current fascination with Oriental religions is a direct Grail quest. The peoples of the East never fractured as Western man did; they never got into or out of the Grail experience so violently. Oriental philosophers regard the West and say, "What in the world is this great push and hunger in your people?"

So their philosophy and point of view are very attractive to us now. But in my estimation it is not very effective for us because it doesn't deal with our situation directly. Westerners can't just "let be" as Orientals can. We are too fragmented to go at it in such a direct way. The Grail myth works more effectively for us because it is rooted in Western psychology.

All of this is an oversimplification, of course. Theoretically a man may visit the Grail castle at any time. He doesn't necessarily come to it just twice. There are moments all along in a man's life when he gets a little bit of the Grail quality. This keeps him going.

If a person were to make a list of the things, places, or circumstances that have brought this quality to him, it would be a revelation. Almost always they are small things—that morning when the toast tasted so good out of the toaster, or that Saturday when he turned the corner and the clouds had a special pattern, or the day someone paid him a bit of a compliment just in passing. It is almost never the big dramatic thing, but the little thing that for just a moment puts him in touch again with the Grail.

The drawbridge is a hint about the nature of the Grail castle. It doesn't exist in physical reality. It is inner reality, a vision. It is poetry, a mystical experience. It is not a specific place. One must know and understand this if he is Grail questing. One of the first things that goes wrong with one's quest is that he expects to find the happiness of the Grail experience with an outer something or in some place. This never works because the Grail isn't a place.

How many men have made how many pilgrimages to particular spots where Grail castles burst open to them in their youth! How many men go back to the place where they grew up, thinking that the place had something to do with their Grail experience!

The Grail castle is an experience that comes at a certain level of consciousness. It is poetic imagery, mystical vision. It does not exist in what is commonly called "reality."

The fact that the drawbridge struck the back feet of the horse is a small but eloquent reminder that entering and leaving the Grail castle are dangerous. Many a youth has been toppled going or coming from the Grail castle. It is not at all uncommon for a youth simply to go to pieces at such a moment. You must be very tender and gentle with a boy when he is going through a Grail castle experience. Don't tease him; he can't stand it.

Theoretically it should be possible for a man to stay in the Grail castle the first time. The Benedictine monks observed this possibility in the days of the monastery. They took boys very young, as babies, raised them in the Grail castle, and never let them out, psychologically speaking. I have never known anyone who had this experience, and I don't think it is possible for modern people, but maybe it worked at one time.

It is important as we go through our story to look at the feminine elements to see what they are doing and then to look at the masculine elements. Some people interpret the whole myth as a war between the masculine bloodshed and the redemptive feminine, but both are brought into balance at the end of the myth in the form of the Grail King.

It is said of the sword that constantly drips blood that it was the sword with which Cain slew Abel and the same sword that pierced Christ's side on the cross. So it is the sword that has done damage in all times, and it bleeds constantly.

Parsifal is torn between his masculine, sword-wielding quality and his feminine Grail hunger. These two interplay constantly. In the Grail castle the sword that drips blood and the Grail are held close together. That represents the unification of the man's aggressive quality with his soul, which searches for love and union. Unless they can be brought into balance these two things create warfare in any man.

The sword is redeemed when it is drawn into the crucifixion and fulfills a holy purpose. This is the case with a man's sword-wielding masculinity. It is redeemed only by suffering. A woman has to wring her hands and keep still when she sees her man heading into a disastrous situation that will bring him into suffering. He has to do it; it is his redemption. If done intelligently, it doesn't need to take very long or cause very much suffering. (But men are not known for intelligence at this point.) So the sword that bleeds is the sword being redeemed by suffering.

This is something not known in the Orient. Oriental philosophers look at our symbolism and say, "Why is there all this gory business involving so much blood?" The moment a culture takes onto itself as much conquest as the Western world has done, it is going to have a bloody sword to cope with. This Aryan, colonizing, domineering thing in our culture springs out of our failure at the Grail castle.

There is a legitimate way of coming back to the Grail castle. There are highly instructive parallels between Christ and the Fisher King. The two stories resemble each other in many ways, with the important difference that the very wise man, Christ, makes the quest the right way. But he still has to go through all the stages. When Christ went to the temple at age twelve and rebuked his parents, this was his first Grail castle, so to speak. He touched something very big—his manhood, his strength. He wasn't badly wounded by it because he understood. He later had to go back to it and was absorbed totally into it. That is the idealized prototype for us to follow. However, I'm especially fond of the twelfth-century Grail myth because it steps it down for us; it is a little bit more human. I can identify with it more directly.

7

Let us return to Parsifal. He has left the Grail castle, and the drawbridge has ticked the back feet of the horse.

He rides on, coming to a sorrowful maiden who has her dead lover in her arms. Her knight was killed when another knight (the lover of the woman of the tent we talked about earlier) went into a rampage when he came back and found that Parsifal had been with his fair damsel. He went right out and slew the first person he could find—this knight. So this knight's death was really Parsifal's fault, and the sorrowing maiden tells Parsifal so in no uncertain terms.

She then asks where he has been. He says that he has been in the local castle. She says there is no castle within thirty miles. He describes the Grail castle, and she says, "Oh, you have been in the Grail castle."

Then she fairly lights into him, berates him terribly, tells him that he did not ask the question as he should have, and so the Grail castle is not relieved of its spell and the illness of the Fisher King is not healed. This, she says, is all Parsifal's fault. She goes through a list of his sins, saying that knights will continue to be slain, maidens will still be bereft, the lands will remain barren, the Fisher King will still suffer, there will be many orphans, and all of this is Parsifal's fault because he didn't ask the proper question.

Then she asks Parsifal who he is. Until this time his name has never been used in the myth. Now he blurts out that his name is Parsifal. Not until Parsifal was in the Grail castle does he have any conception of who he is. He had no sense of his individual identity before, but after he has been in the Grail castle he knows who he is.

Parsifal goes on. In due time he comes to the maiden of the tent. She is sitting in rags and mourning. Her knight has treated her badly ever since Parsifal blundered into her tent. The maiden tells Parsifal to go away because her knight will kill Parsifal if he comes along. Then she too reiterates his misdeed in not asking the crucial question in the Grail castle. Her knight does come back, but Parsifal subdues him in a duel and sends him off to Arthur's court. (There is an endless stream of knights sent back to Arthur's court by Parsifal. Perhaps it is important not to end a neurosis until we have overcome enough within ourselves.) The weeping damsel then tells Parsifal that the sword which was given him in the castle will break the first time he uses it in battle, that it is not trustworthy. She says that it can only be mended by the smith who made it. However, she says, when it is repaired it will never break again.

This is a boy's normal experience. The masculinity a boy uses at first comes from his father. It breaks the first time he uses it. He goes out and tries to do something the way his dad did it, but it doesn't work. It is only an imitation. It takes another father—a spiritual father, a godfather—to repair it. Then it is good, and it will hold up the rest of his life.

Now so many conquered knights have turned up at Arthur's castle that the whole court is in a turmoil over this hero whom they didn't recognize before. They want Parsifal to come to Arthur's castle and be the great man of the day in Arthur's court. But they don't know where he is. So Arthur sets forth to search for Parsifal. Arthur vows he will not sleep twice in the same bed until he finds this magnificent hero, the greatest knight of all time. Parsifal is camping not far from Arthur's court, but he is not aware of it.

Then a very curious thing happens, one of the most puzzling things in the myth. A falcon attacks three geese in the air and wounds one of them; three drops of blood fall from the wounded goose onto the snow. When Parsifal sees this, he is immediately reminded of Blanche Fleur, whom he hasn't thought of for some time. Parsifal is always forgetting somebody. He goes off on a tangent and forgets. How many adolescents have come home with a sudden dawn of recognition—"Oh, I forgot. I got interested in something else and I forgot!"

There are three drops of blood in the snow, and Parsifal falls into a lover's trance, remembering his fair lady. He just sits there staring at the drops of blood on the snow. Two of Arthur's men see Parsifal at this moment. They recognize him and try to convince him to come back to Arthur's court. In Parsifal's strange lover's trance, and with his extraordinary knightly power, he unhorses first one and then the other. The second knight has his arm broken. Incidentally, he is the knight who had insulted the maiden who hadn't laughed for six years. Remember when she laughed one of the knights insulted her and threw Parsifal into the fire? Parsifal swore he would avenge this. Suddenly, the legend is beginning to pull together. The maiden is now avenged!

A third knight, Gawain, appears. He asks Parsifal very gently and humbly if he will come back to Arthur's court with him, and Parsifal agrees.

Another version of this curious section of the story has it that the sun came out and melted the snow enough so that two of the three drops of blood disappear and Parsifal is released so that he can function again and can go to Arthur's court.

Now this is a strange bit of mythology we have in our hands: Blanche Fleur, the snow, three drops of blood, Parsifal suddenly waking from his trance. If the sun hadn't melted two of the drops of blood, Parsifal might have been immobilized forever.

Numbers in mythology and dreams are often highly instructive. Remember how many fours there were in the Grail castle? This was telling us in symbolic language that the Grail castle was a place of wholeness, a place that had the character of the quaternity. Four seems to represent completeness, peace, stability, timelessness.

Three, on the other hand, represents urgency, incompleteness, restlessness, and striving. I think I see a play on the completeness of the Grail castle experience and the incompleteness of Parsifal's immediate human relationship with Blanche Fleur. They are both good, but I think they are telling us that the Blanche Fleur experience is a powerful but partial system and the Grail experience is a total system, embracing everything.

When one is in the dilemma of three, if one is struggling with three, he must increase it to four or reduce it to one; these are the only bearable solutions or possibilities. Parsifal can't get back to the Grail castle. He can't go from the symbolism of three to the symbolism of four. So the next best thing is to reduce the symbol to one and then he can function again.

Sometimes if one is in a paralyzing dilemma, he must reduce his consciousness a bit just in order to function. If he can go ahead, can progress to the next number, then of course this is the best of all. But if he can't, he must regress a little just to save himself and function again.

Two is bad because one gets stuck in its duality. One and four are workable. Two and three are difficult, unstable, incomplete; they are stages one has to go through and are worthy of one's respect, but one may not tarry there.

The implications of this number symbolism may also relate to the Christian doctrine of the Trinity. This is a thorny subject and I don't want to go very far with it, but it would seem that the Trinitarian view of man's nature, or the Godhead, is incomplete. The threeness of God requires the inclusion of the fourth to achieve completeness and stability. Anytime one has a Trinitarian system going there will be an adversary somewhere, for something will have been left out. What has been rejected will reappear as the devil, for whenever something of the spirit that belongs to wholeness is excluded it turns against us. Jung has made quite a bit of this and often suggests that what has been excluded from the Christian Trinity is the dark, feminine element in life. So it comes back to plague us as a kind of chthonic devil.

We are apparently in an age where the consciousness of man is advancing from a Trinitarian to a quaternitarian view. This is one possible and profound way of talking about the extreme chaos our world is now in. One hears many dreams of modern people, who, knowing nothing consciously of this number symbolism, dream of three turning into four. This suggests we are going through an evolution of consciousness. From the nice, orderly, all-masculine concept of ultimate reality, the Trinitarian view of God, we are moving toward a quaternitarian view that includes the feminine, as well as other elements that are pretty difficult to include if one insists on a system of perfection.

For it seems that it is God's purpose now to replace an image of perfection with completion or wholeness. Perfection suggests something all pure with no blemishes, dark spots, or questionable areas. Wholeness includes even the darkness but combines the dark elements with the light elements into a totality. Generally speaking, the Christian striving has been toward goodness and perfection, not toward wholeness and completion. The movement toward wholeness is a formidable task, for it always involves us in paradox. I am not at all sure that mankind is capable of that task right now, but it seems to be thrust upon us anyway.

Jung rightly suggests that the 1950 dogma of the bodily assumption of the Virgin Mary into heaven is the dogmatic statement of the quarternity. Mary in her body now lives in majesty in heaven. Taken literally this is all nonsense, but taken psychologically it is important, for it is the inclusion of the earthy, feminine element in the heavenly Trinity. Now there are no longer just three male aspects of God; a fourth and feminine element is added. Femininity is belatedly recognized as an element worthy of reigning forever with God. Jung was jubilant about the dogma of bodily assumption of the Virgin Mary in heaven. But it has come and gone and has been mostly forgotten and hardly anyone has noticed. But if one can hear this extraordinary event in the right way, there may be hope for the Church. The feminine, the fourth element, is added to the Trinity. If we can follow the guidance laid out for us, then there is hope for the future.

As soon as the fourth element is given dignity and status, it is no longer the adversary. It is an adversary only when it is excluded. Then it pounds on the door, so to speak, to get in and, naturally, looks like evil to us. It is we who make the elements devilish by excluding them. It is a general principle that anything rejected from one's psyche becomes hostile. If one understands this, one is well on the way to knowing what to do about it.

What a man sees as the evil element is often the feminine side. When the man's feminine side is excluded, he often gets witchy. Much of the darkness of the rejected element during the Middle Ages was feminine, hence all the witch hunting. Witch hunting was not just an isolated incident here and there that got a lot of publicity. At the height of the witch hunting there were more than 4 million women burned at the stake in Europe. This was because the dark, feminine element was seen in such a negative light. Now we hold our breath to see if this seemingly dangerous element can be included in the general psychic economy. It can't be done naively because inclusion of the rejected side is a dangerous operation. If one has antagonized the wolf, then one doesn't just suddenly open the door and say, "Now, come on in."

8

Parsifal is escorted in triumph to Arthur's court. He is the lion of the day; he is the greatest knight who ever lived. Celebration and great festivities go on for three days. One could hardly wish for anything better. To be the head of Arthur's court is the ultimate in knighthood. So now Parsifal is head man, top of the heap in Arthur's court. Then, on a decrepit old mule that limps on all four feet, in comes a hideous damsel. I have to quote the description: "Her black hair was tressed in two braids, iron dark were her hands and nails. Her closed eyes small like a rat's. Her nose like an ape and cat. Her lips like an ass and bull. Bearded was she, humped breast and back, her loins and shoulders twisted like roots of a tree. Never in royal court was such a damsel seen."

The hideous damsel rides into the camp on her mule, stops everything cold, and recites all of Parsifal's sins. She recites in detail what he didn't do in the Grail castle, why he didn't do it, the plight of the king because of this, and then she says that it is all Parsifal's fault. She tells long stories about the knights that have already been slain because of Parsifal's failure, the weeping damsels, the devastated lands, the orphaned children.

Then she points an accusing finger at Parsifal and says, "It is all your fault."

This is the hideous damsel. This usually happens at the very apex of a man's career, at the time of his greatest success. He has just been named president of the corporation, has just been elected to the academy, has just made his first million, or whatever the apex of life is for him, and within three days the hideous damsel will walk in on him.

This is the anima gone absolutely sour and dark. There is some correlation between the amount of fame and adulation one gets in the outer world and the condition of the anima. They often have an inverse relationship to one another. When a man really succeeds, then he is often in for trouble with his anima.

I am told that the technical term for this is *involutional melancholia.* I prefer to call it the hideous damsel. It is much more descriptive. But she serves an excellent purpose, and a man can learn much at this point. In fact, he must learn if he is to get beyond his depression.

This is that destroying, spoiling quality in a man at about middle age. Suddenly the savor has gone out of everything. The hideous damsel whispers in his ears, "What is the use of going to the office? What difference does it make? What good is it? What does it all mean?" The wife has long since ceased being the anima for him. The children are either difficult or gone. The new boat isn't as invigorating as he thought it was going to be. The last vacation didn't work very well. He is just "turning the crank." These are all manifestations of the hideous damsel.

A man often comes down with a series of vague complaints at this time. His stomach is an appropriate organ for the hideous damsel. He is also very likely to try a new mistress. The term *fatal forties* is accurate, I think. When the hideous damsel lands upon one, it is just about fatal to try to dispel her by getting some new fair damsel.

So this is Parsifal's experience of the hideous damsel. The court is absolutely stricken by this. No one argues with her. No one has anything to say because it is all true.

Then she begins to parcel out tasks to the 466 knights in Arthur's court. (These explicit numbers in myth are often highly illuminating and sometimes equally highly puzzling. I don't know what in the world to do with 466. But there are 466 knights, for the edification of your unconscious, even if we can't understand consciously.) One she sends off to lift a siege from a castle, another to slay a tiresome dragon in the next country. She sends everybody off, each on his task.

Each knight goes off alone. All group activity stops at this moment. It becomes an individual quest. Each man has his own quest. They are forbidden to take their wives or their fair maidens with them. They go riding off alone.

Perhaps our culture can begin to understand this part of the myth when enough individuals have dispersed under the command of the hideous damsel, gone through their quest, and made their way back to the Grail castle. But I don't think the problem can ever be solved collectively. For better or worse we are individuals, and our way is an individual way. That is why the great collective moves are so ineffective. I regret this, because it makes it so hard, but it seems to be so.

The hideous damsel sends Parsifal off to search for the Grail castle for the second time. Parsifal swears a holy vow that he will not sleep in the same bed two nights running until he has found the Grail castle.

So here we learn what we must do with the hideous damsel when she comes. She is useful. You must not take tranquilizers and tell her to go away. You must not try to banish her with another fair damsel. You must not try to hide from her. You must not try to argue her down. When we men are forty or fifty and the hideous damsel turns up and makes her devastating accusations, we must not try to wriggle out of it. It is the universal impulse to try to get out of the accusations of the hideous damsel, but this is absolutely the wrong thing to do. You must stick with her. You must just sit there and take it as long as she chooses to sit there on her mule and outline your faults. Because when she has gone through her long speech, she will then set you on your quest again. This is what she is for.

This is also a good time for a flesh-and-blood woman to be very, very quiet. First, so that she won't be saddled with the man's projection of the hideous damsel, which the man would be only too happy to put on her. Second, so that the man can get his bearings and learn from the devastating experience. If he can keep faith with the hideous damsel, she will tell him what he has to do. She will sternly order him to continue the search.

So all the knights of Arthur's court are sent off on

their many quests. Then comes a repetition of the injunction that the knights must remain chaste. I remind you for the hundredth time that this hasn't anything to do with what one is doing with flesh-and-blood woman. This is a chaste relationship with that interior woman, who is more easily identified with one's feeling side or, God forbid, one's moody side.

So all of the knights are told that they must not seduce or be seduced if they are to see the Grail. And they all fail except Parsifal. Many of the 11,000 lines of the poem pursue various knights, their glorious deeds, and their ultimate fall from grace.

There are so many fallings from grace. This means that many, many parts of a man go out on a quest but succumb to an anima possession. Many parts of a man fall into a mood, or get trapped, or get locked into an anima dilemma. But a central part of the man, the Parsifal in him, may remember, understand, and finally make his way through to the Grail in the end.

9

Parsifal goes on through innumerable episodes. Some versions of the myth have it that he travels for five years; others say twenty years. All manner of things happen. He grows more bitter, more disillusioned; he gets harder and harder. He is farther and farther from his Blanche Fleur, his feminine consciousness. He forgets why he is wielding the sword. He conquers knights right and left, but for less and less reason and with less joy within himself.

Then he comes across a band of ragged pilgrims who are wandering along. They say to him, "What in the world are you doing riding around at full tilt like this on Good Friday?" And he says, "Is it Good Friday?"

Suddenly Parsifal remembers. In a reverie, he remembers what his mother taught him about the church. He remembers Blanche Fleur. He remembers the Grail castle. He is stricken with nostalgia and remorse. He asks the pilgrims where they are going and they say, "To a hermit for Good Friday confession." Parsifal joins them.

They make their way to the hut of a hermit, who turns out to be Parsifal's uncle, his father's brother who has become a monk.

The hermit is the introverted part of one's masculine heritage. When all of one's masculine activities are extraverted, five or twenty years of extraversion are of no avail. Finally one sees that he isn't going to be able to work his way through this dilemma. One sees that the second million or the second wife or whatever extraverted activities he pursues aren't going to solve the problem. Then he turns to his own introverted hermit living in the woods in a little hut; that is where he gets the next bit of strength or power.

This is the time for a man to take six weeks off from his job and go away to summon that hermit in himself, that extremely introverted sum of energy within him. This will give him the perspective he needs for the next stage of life. People often do this against their will by going to the hospital. They get ill and go to the hospital where they are absolutely immobile, but they come out of it over the hump. It is a rough way to do it, but if one doesn't understand the introversion that is needed and do it consciously, it may be the only way to get an active man to lie down.

The hermit also represents another way a boy may follow besides the Red Knight way. Ordinarily the boy goes through the Red Knight stage, gains his strength, goes out, and wields his sword. But there is another way. A few boys—quiet, introverted souls—go the hermit's way. This is also legitimate. One must understand if he goes the hermit's way that he ask nothing of the Red Knight experience. He mustn't ask for the laurel leaves of victory. He mustn't expect top place, a position in the community. Symbolically he has to go to a hut in the woods and live alone quietly. But this *is* a way.

The hermit's way is not so torn into opposites. He doesn't lose the Grail castle so completely and devastatingly as Parsifal does. Although it is not uncommon for Red Knight fathers to have hermit sons, the hermit way is still rare. If you have such a son, don't ever push him into the Red Knight experience. His way is different.

This is much simplified, of course. Actually, everyone goes both ways. A part of every man goes the hermit's way, for instance, when a man wanders off for half a day and wants to be alone. Everybody is part hermit, and everybody gets on his charger sometimes to go dashing off. So it is closer to reality to say that each man has both of these elements within him. It is wise to tend both.

So we find Parsifal with the hermit. Although Parsifal hasn't said a word, the hermit begins to recite all of Parsifal's faults, the whole long list. It is apparently written all over him. The hermit tells Parsifal that it is because of his mother that all of this has happened, but he tells him gently without reprimanding him.

Parsifal has failed to treat his mother correctly. But he has also followed her advice too slavishly. This is an invariable characteristic of the mother complex, that it leads to too much and too little all at the same moment.

So Parsifal's mother complex has prevented him from freeing the Grail castle from its spell. The hermit gives Parsifal absolution and tells him that he must go now immediately to the Grail castle. We find then that Parsifal is capable of going for the second time to the Grail castle.

Here the great French poem stops. Some people feel that the author died, was interrupted, or that part of the manuscript was lost. I am more inclined to believe that he stopped where he was. He couldn't say any more. And in many ways he stopped exactly where we are.

This is a myth for our time. It is not yet finished. We have to finish it. We have to carry it on. Even though we don't talk about Grails and castles and enchanted maidens, still it is our myth to be completed in our lives. The myth has taken us exactly to the point where modern people are now. Collectively speaking, we are stuck at the point where the French poem ends. So if you want a quest, if you want something meaningful for your life, pick up the Grail myth where it now lies in you.

10

Other authors tried to finish this myth after Chrétien de Troyes. None of these endings is satisfactory or convincing. Maybe this is because the myth has not progressed in our souls any farther than the French poem. But let's look at these endings anyway and see what we can learn.

According to some versions of the myth, Parsifal makes his way immediately to the Grail castle. He sees. He understands. Now, it is true that as soon as a man knows about the Grail castle consciously, and as soon as he is humble enough and courageous enough, he can go immediately to it. No amount of swashbuckling about will get him there. But if he asks for the Grail castle with all his heart, he finds it immediately.

Parsifal finds the drawbridge and goes over. It is exactly the same as it was before; the Fisher King is still suffering. After the necessary formalities, Parsifal asks the question, "Whom does the Grail serve?" The answer is given him immediately, "The Grail serves the Grail King."

A strange answer. The Grail King is not the Fisher King. The Grail King lives in the central room of the castle. He has lived there from time immemorial. He worships the Grail constantly, is fed by the Grail, and has nothing to do with anything but the Grail. He worships it, he tends it. He and the Grail are in constant communion and exchange.

So here is the answer to the perplexing question that has dogged us all this time. Whom does the Grail serve? The Grail serves the Grail King.

I have lived with this answer to the question for months and slowly evolved some understanding of it. Almost everybody in our culture thinks that the Grail is to serve us, but here there is something essential to learn. The great search for most Americans is for happiness—which is to say that we ask the Grail to serve us. We ask that this great cornucopia of nature, this great feminine outpouring, all of the material of the world—the air, the sea, the animals, the oil, the forests, and all the productivity of the world—we assume that it should serve us. And the lesson that we have to learn is that this cornucopia of nature does not serve us; it serves God.

The Grail King is the image of God, the earthly representation of the divine. The myth is telling us that our task is to learn that the Grail serves the Grail King, not that the Grail serves us. As in the recent myth, *The Fellowship of the Ring* by J. R. R. Tolkien, the power must be taken from those who would exploit it. In the Grail myth the source of power is given to the representative of God. In the Tolkien myth the ring of power is taken from evil hands and put back into the ground from which it came. Earlier myths often spoke of the discovery of power and its emergence from the earth into human hands. Recent myths speak of returning the source of power to the earth or into the hands of God before we destroy ourselves with it.

We are not prepared yet to hear this change that is required of us, but there are the beginnings of consciousness in this direction. The ring is our modern self-conscious power, our science. We must relinquish this power, this brave new world we have around us, or it will destroy us.

I think the modern form of the great question, a form that would be meaningful to us, is "What do we live for?" As soon as one asks that question and has the courage to hear the answer, one has a surprise in store that will heal the Fisher King wound in him.

The object of life is not happiness, but to serve God or the Grail. All of the Grail involvements are to serve God. If one understands this and drops his idiotic notion that the meaning of life is personal happiness, then one will be flooded with happiness.

The myth says that as Parsifal asks the question, the Fisher King is immediately healed. Rejoicing begins in the Grail castle. The Grail is brought forth. It gives its food to everyone, and there is perfect peace, joy, and well-being. Here is this incredible dilemma: If you ask for the Grail to make you happy, you have precluded happiness. If you will serve the Grail and the Grail King properly, you will be flooded with happiness.

Alexis de Tocqueville, a Frenchman who came to America more than a century ago, made some astute observations about the American temperament, atmosphere, and idiom. He said that we have a misleading idea in our Constitution, the pursuit of happiness. One can't pursue happiness; it won't work.

A formulation for these days could go something like this: "If you will serve your reality, you will be flooded with happiness. But if you merely search for happiness, you will dispel the very happiness for which you are looking."

There are terrible things going on about which the Grail myth could enlighten us. It could lead us out of some dilemmas. We are just beginning to ask, for example, if we have the right to poison the air and cut down all the trees and pump all the oil and kill all the pelicans. We are just beginning to ask the Grail question: "What is this all for? Is it only for us?"

The Grail myth suggests the only possible answer to that question: We must manage the things of the earth for the glory of God, not for man or a superman. If one could ask the question "Whom does the Grail serve?" if one could evolve consciousness to understand what this question means, he would take it very seriously and ask it in full consciousness. Then he would find out. The answer is immediate once the question is asked. Then a false search for happiness stops, and a flood of happiness comes.

This is where we are. This is the next evolution of mankind required of us. We are just on the edge of it. We are just lisping out the first syllable of that great question which will heal all of us Fisher Kings.

And so, with Parsifal, we've made a long journey, a round trip—from the Garden of Eden to the heavenly Jerusalem, from Grail castle to Grail castle. With Parsifal we have learned that we must ask the great question, "Whom does the Grail serve?" And we must not just assume that it serves us. We have an intimation of the answer to the great question of the meaning of life itself, if we have journeyed far enough and have enough consciousness to hear and understand that answer.

Appendix: Synopsis of the Grail Legend

According to Chrétien de Troyes

The Holy Grail, the chalice of the Last Supper, is kept within a castle. The king of the castle has been severely wounded and suffers continuously because his wound will not heal. The entire country and its people are in desolation.

The king had been wounded early in his adolescence. While wandering in a forest, he had reached a camp that was empty except for a spit on which a salmon was roasting. He was hungry, so he took a bit of the salmon. He burned his fingers horribly. To assuage the pain, he put his fingers into his mouth and tasted a bit of the salmon. He is called the Fisher King because he was wounded by a fish. He was also wounded in the thighs, so he is no longer productive, and his whole land is no longer productive. The Fisher King lies on a litter and must be carried everywhere, but he is sometimes able to fish, and only then is he happy.

The Fisher King presides over the castle where the Grail is kept, but he cannot touch the Grail or be healed by it. The court fool has prophesied that the Fisher King would be healed when a wholly innocent fool arrives in the court.

In an isolated country a boy lives with his widowed mother, whose name is Heart Sorrow. At first the boy does not seem to have a name; much later he learns that his name is Parsifal. His father had been killed while rescuing a fair maiden, and his two brothers had also been killed as knights. His mother had taken him to this faraway country and raised him in primitive circumstances. He wears homespun clothes, has no schooling, asks no questions. He is a simple, naive youth.

Early in his adolescence, he sees five knights riding by on horseback. He is dazzled by the knights, their scarlet-and-gold trappings, their armor, and all their accoutrements. He dashes home to tell his mother that he has seen five gods and wants to leave home to go with them.

His mother weeps. She had hoped that he would not suffer the fate of his father and his brothers. But she gives him her blessing and three instructions: He must respect all fair maidens; he is to go daily to church where he will receive all the food he needs; and he is not to ask any questions.

Parsifal goes off to find the knights. He never finds the same five knights, but he has all kinds of adventures. One day he comes to a tent. He had only known a simple hut, so he thinks this is the church his mother had told him about. He sees a fair damsel wearing a ring on her hand, so he obeys his mother's instruction by embracing the damsel, taking her ring, and putting it on his own hand. He sees a table set for a banquet and, thinking it is the food his mother had told him he would find in church, he eats it, not realizing it is prepared for the damsel's beloved knight. The damsel begs Parsifal to leave, because if her knight finds him there he will kill him.

Parsifal goes on his way and soon finds a devastated convent and monastery. He cannot restore them, but he vows to return and raise the spell when he is stronger.

Then he meets a Red Knight who has come from King Arthur's Court. Parsifal is dazzled by the knight and tells him that he too wants to be a knight. The Red Knight tells him to go to Arthur's court, which he does. In this court is a damsel who has not smiled or laughed for six years. A legend says that when the best knight in the world comes along, she will smile and laugh again. When she sees Parsifal, she bursts into laughter. The court is impressed. Arthur knights Parsifal, gives him a page, and tells him that he may have the horse and armor of the Red Knight if he can get it.

Parsifal finds the Red Knight, kills him, and takes his armor and puts it on over his homespun clothing. He finds his way to the castle of Gournamond, who trains him to be a knight. Gournamond gives him two instructions: He must never seduce or be seduced by a woman, and when he reaches the Grail castle he must ask, "Whom does the Grail serve?"

Parsifal goes off and tries to find his mother and help her, but he finds that she died of a broken heart. Then he meets Blanche Fleur. From this time on, everything he does is in her service. She asks him to conquer the army besieging her castle, which he does, and then he spends the night with her.

After traveling all of the next day, he meets two men in a boat. One of them, who is fishing, invites Parsifal to stay at his house for the night. When Parsifal reaches this house, he finds himself in a great castle, where he is royally welcomed. He learns that the fisherman is the Fisher King. He sees a ceremony in which a youth carries a sword that drips blood constantly and in which a maiden carries the Grail. At a banquet the Grail is passed about and everyone drinks from it. The Fisher King's niece brings a sword, and the King straps it to Parsifal's waist. But Parsifal fails to ask the question Gournamond had told him to ask. The next morning Parsifal finds that all the people of the castle have vanished. Then the castle itself disappears.

He goes on and finds a sorrowful maiden. He learns that her knight had been killed by the jealous knight of the maiden of the tent, so the death was really his fault. When she learns that he has been in the Grail castle, she berates him for all his sins and tells him that the land and its people will continue to be desolate because he failed to ask the right question.

Later he again finds the maiden of the tent. She reiterates all his misdeeds and tells him that the sword he had been given will break the first time it is used in battle, that it can only be mended by the smith who made it, and that after that it will never break again.

In the course of his journeys, Parsifal has subdued many knights and sent them back to King Arthur's Court. When he had been there before, they had not realized who he was. Arthur sets forth to search for Parsifal so the court can honor him. Parsifal happens to be camping nearby. A falcon attacks three geese and wounds one of them. Its blood on the snow reminds Parsifal of Blanche Fleur, and he falls into a trance. Two of Arthur's men see him and try to persuade him to return to the court, but he unhorses them. A third knight, Gawain, gently persuades him to go to the court with him. Parsifal is received in triumph at the court.

But the rejoicing ends when a hideous damsel on a decrepit mule enters and recites all of Parsifal's sins. Then she points a finger at him and says, "It is all your fault." She assigns tasks to all the knights. She tells Parsifal to search for the Grail castle again and this time ask the right question.

Parsifal goes on through many episodes. Some versions say that he travels for five years; others say twenty years. He grows bitter and disillusioned. He does many heroic deeds, but he forgets the church, Blanche Fleur, and the Grail castle.

Then one day he meets some pilgrims who ask him why he is armed on Good Friday. He suddenly remembers what he had forgotten. Remorsefully he goes with the pilgrims to a hermit for confession. The hermit absolves him and tells him to go immediately to the Grail castle.

The poem by Chrétien de Troyes stops here. Many authors tried to finish it. One version says that Parsifal goes to the Grail castle and this time he asks the right question: "Whom does the Grail serve?" The answer is given: "The Grail serves the Grail King." He is not the Fisher King, but the Grail King, who has lived in the central room of the castle from time immemorial. The Fisher King is healed immediately, and the land and all its people can live in peace and joy.

Bibliography

THE BASIC REFERENCE

Jung, Emma, and Von Franz, Marie-Louise. *The Grail Legend*. A C. G. Jung Foundation Book. New York: G. P. Putnam's Sons, 1970.

RELATED WORKS

Campbell, Joseph. *The Hero with a Thousand Faces*. Princeton: Princeton University Press, 1968.
———. *Myths to Live By*. New York: Viking Press, Inc., 1973.
———, ed. *The Portable Jung*. New York: Viking Press, Inc., 1976.
Jung, Carl G. *Man and His Symbols*. Garden City, N.Y.: Doubleday, 1969.
———. *Memories, Dreams, Reflections*. New York: Random House, Inc., 1961.
Kelsey, Morton T. *Encounter with God*. Minneapolis, Minn.: Bethany Fellowship, Inc., 1972.
Sanford, John A. *Dreams: God's Forgotten Language*. Philadelphia: J. B. Lippincott Co., 1968.
———. *The Kingdom Within*. Philadelphia: J. B. Lippincott Co., 1970.
———. *The Man Who Wrestled with God*. Ramsey, N.J.: Paulist Press, 1981.
Whitmont, Edward C. *The Symbolic Quest*. Princeton: Princeton University Press, 1978.